II Peter 1:2-10
Verse 2 - Grace and p[e...]
Through the knowledge o[f ...]
Lord.
blessings.

An
Olive Branch
from
Lebanon

From Oosanna
or
Hosanna
Allen

Matthew 6:33

THE TESTIMONY OF
HOSANNA ALLEN

An
Olive Branch
from
Lebanon

THE TESTIMONY OF HOSANNA ALLEN
MATLOCK – DERBYSHIRE – UK

Expression
NOTTINGHAM, ENGLAND

Published by Expression

Nottingham, England

First published in the UK in 2005

Expression is an imprint of New Life Publishing

Copyright © Ovsanna Allen

ISBN 9780-9536100-7-1

Printed by Creative Print and Design Group, Middlesex, England

All Scripture references in this book are taken from
the New International Version (NIV)
unless otherwise stated.
Copyright © International Bible Society.

Contents

Acknowledgements

I offer my special thanks and appreciation to Catherine Sauzier, a computing teacher, who gave her precious time and skills in checking and printing, to the extent of exhausting her computer ink cartridge! To Judy England for coming over in all weathers to proof read with her teacher's detective ability. Many thanks to Renee Macpherson for her speedy help. Above all to Rhoda Carswell's sound advice. Thank you, I am grateful to you all.

I dedicate this story

to my sons:

Daniel, Samuel, Timothy and Paul.

Also to all my extended family and friends.

Foreword

I realised only recently that I have known Hosanna for around 40 years. I have happy memories of helping to give a bottle to one of her twins, whilst she fed the other one. I also remember with amusement the time she visited us when Timothy was a toddler. He was reluctant to go indoors, so she hinted to him that if he stayed outdoors in the field, my father-in-law's cattle that were grazing there might like to "eat him up". He scampered indoors really quickly! Over the decades I have seen all her four boys grow into adulthood and excel in the various careers which they have chosen.

Hosanna and I have had many happy hours of fellowship together, but the times I have enjoyed most have been the ones when she has shared little snippets of her life story, and the lives of her Armenian family and friends before she came to live in England. So I am really delighted that at last she has had the time to put some of these memories into the form of this book.

As you read this short autobiography, I am sure it will sometimes be with a smile and sometimes a tear, but always with great interest.

Judy England

Introduction

David the Psalmist describes my heart's gratitude to God in Psalm 40:5: "Many, O LORD my God, are the wonders you have done. The things you planned for us no one can recount to you; were I to speak and tell of them, they would be too many to declare." In Psalm 139:5-6 I read, "You hem me in – behind and before; you have laid your hand upon me. Such knowledge is too wonderful for me, too lofty for me to attain."

His tangible presence has followed me throughout my life and because of an awareness of His presence in my life, the tempter has never been too far away to trouble me. God says, "Because of His mercy we are not consumed." We are told to call on Him in the day of trouble and He hears and delivers us from it all: "No temptation has seized you except what is common to man. And God is faithful; He will not let you be tempted beyond what you can bear. But when you are tempted, He will also provide a way out so that you can stand up under it" (1 Corinthians 10:13).

I gave my life to Jesus at the age of nine. I've have had ups and downs but He carried me upon His shoulders. I sought the Lord through it all. The verse Matthew 6:33 became my life's motto. I followed God's leading. He put in me the desire to seek Him and serve Him. He guided, protected and provided. All praise to Jesus.

People have often asked me how and why I came to England. This gave me the opportunity to give my testimony as I had a valid reason. It gave me great pleasure to tell others the wonders that God himself has performed on my behalf.

Last year at my son's ordination as pastor at FGCC in Boston, Massachusetts, a magazine was handed to me. On the front page I read, "Reading, Writing and Ridicule – a college president tells how he overcame disability and ridicule". When I read the contents of his testimony, his experience at school, it almost matched mine. Encouraged by this article I was prompted to write my testimony.

Secondly, just a few weeks before leaving Wayland, MA, a friend called Eliz from Montreal, a young worship leader, came to spend a few days at my son's house. We had a wonderful time of sharing the good things the Lord has done for us. We prayed earnestly that God would enable us to write our testimony and declare His mighty deeds.

Thirdly, after my return home to Matlock in Derbyshire, I was reading 'Word for Today' by Bob Gass and it said, "Just tell your story. Acts 1:8 says, 'You will be my witnesses.' Act on your thoughts before the expiry date." I could no longer keep it to myself. I knew it was the will of God to put my words onto paper.

The main reason for writing this autobiography is to give glory to His matchless abounding grace.

1
Life in Karantina

Father had a two-storey house built in Karantina in preparation for his marriage to Yeghsapet Varjabedian, a 16-year-old young lady with blue eyes and tender complexion, chosen from amongst hundreds of Armenian refugees from Turkey.

Dad's house was one of a few brick buildings in the area. An hour-and-a-half walking distance from the harbour, it stood elegantly along the seashore about half a mile inland. This area had several army barracks: military training department buildings for storing military supplies, with large fields for army exercises. One third of this area was allocated for the homeless refugees, mostly Armenians, who had arrived from Turkish exile. Temporary shelters were constructed for them to live in. Dad married soon after the house was ready.

This district, where we lived for a few years, was called 'Karantina'. A portion of the land was set apart for isolation purposes, 'quarantine', to prevent the spread of infectious diseases. This area occupied the central part of the East Mediterranean and was securely fenced in with high walls, as well as with barbed wire.

Some of the immigrants who came to Beirut to travel abroad, needing a limited period of quarantine, were sent here to recover or get over the incubation period. In order not to carry infectious diseases elsewhere, the ships' crews too were subjected to this regime. There was also a Military Hospital with extensive rows of makeshift shelters. The immigrants who had come to Beirut Harbour, from all over the Middle East, were housed in those corrugated iron shelters, and there was very poor sanitation within the camp.

Some adventurous men tried to escape during the night, but some fell to their death, and some were caught. We read about these in the newspaper. While some were trying to get out, other naughty boys would try to climb in from the outside, but they never succeeded. Apart from being hurt and tearing their garments, climbing those treacherous barbed wire fences presented a challenge for many young teenagers, just as any prohibited thing poses a tremendous temptation. The fact was that in those days children had no toys to play with as they have today. The luxury of computer games or television did not exist.

Mr Khacher married Miss Yeghsapet in 1926. Both began to contribute towards their home life to make it a successful happy marriage. They let some of the rooms to tenants in order to bring in money; father worked at the Beirut Harbour canteen. Soon the family started to arrive and by 1937 they had three children, and were happily settled in Beirut's Karantina region.

The political atmosphere was in turmoil, the air was full of rumours of the Second World War. Things began to change, Dad was moved to Tel Aviv with the French Military connection and was employed as kitchen staff. He left behind an expectant mother who had to manage all on her own, bringing up her three young children, as well as doing part-time laundry work at the harbour, doing the washing for the marines as they came onshore from their war activities.

The eldest daughter, Naomi, who was ten years old became, as it were, the foster mother of her two brothers, Hagop, seven years old, and Bedros, under two years of age. She had to shoulder the heavy responsibility of looking after her brothers. Another of her tasks included kneading the dough, leaving it to rise, then taking it to the communal oven to be baked, so that when Mother returned from the harbour launderette, tired and exhausted, she would find freshly baked loaves of bread for all to enjoy eating together, and Mum would have quality time with her children.

During my dad's absence my mother was heavily pregnant, still walking to and from the harbour launderette. The long hours of washing made her fingers look like squashed raisins. Mother had passed the responsibility of caring for the family to Naomi, including household chores. Naomi gladly took on the responsibility. Nothing was too hard or impossible for her, and she was looking forward to this baby's arrival. These were very hard days, but she seemed to have mastered the fostering of her brothers.

My birth

One unexpected daybreak, Mother summoned her daughter to go and call the midwife, who lived some distance away. By the time they arrived, the baby was born in the kitchen in a large bathtub, most likely in the full gaze of the bewildered brothers. I had started my journey in this life.

As soon as Mother heard the cry of her baby daughter, she named her Ovsanna (a very common Armenian name). The English translation is 'Hosanna'. In the Hebrew language its meaning is 'save us now' (reference Matthew 21:9). My mother chose the name in memory of her massacred sister who had been killed by Turkish rebels towards the end of the First World War.

Confusion over my date of birth!

Incidentally, no one remembered my date of birth. I once over-heard them negotiating my date of birth – apparently on that very special day there had been a funeral in the district of Karantina. The funerals were well attended by most of the living, as were the weddings, as a matter of tradition. This funeral was different: it was a well-loved priest's funeral, so it drew the whole community. This national grief and lamentation must have created a lot of stress and pressure, so much so that the priest who was conducting the funeral service collapsed in the cemetery and died during the interment. The incident made an indelible impression on all those who were present in the cemetery – it left them with lasting memories of fear and possibly judgement to come. This special day was 10th February 1938, and so my date of birth was fixed as such.

I lately received a telephone call from my cousin in Nevada, California. In the course of our social conversation, he asked me how old I was. When I told him what I believed to be my age, he was surprised to hear that I was a year older than he thought. I do remember my dad also querying the year of my birth, but he did nothing to change it. It should have been recorded as 1939, not 1938; but since it was during the blitz, there were more pressing needs. My birth date was not registered by the midwife, nor by my parents, and it is too late now to make any change.

My birth during the blitz must have been a novelty for my cousins. One said, "You were as big as my palm." Another said, "You were no bigger than the lamp bulb." Mother said, "Save us now." Baby said, "Gee ." However, what difference does it make now? The line has been drawn by my ten-year-old sister's testimony, no change can be implemented so late in my life.

The death of Ovsanna Varjabedian, my aunt

During the uprising of the First World War, countless numbers of Armenians were exiled. It has been estimated that about one-and-a-half million were massacred for their love of Christ. Many who would not deny Jesus stood true to their testimony and were strong in their love of Christ. They resisted the power of the enemy; they were not afraid of the sword of death; they loved the Lord more than life and possessions, because the Lord was all in all to them. Thousands of books have been written about those who escaped through death and by those who were told the stories by parents who had survived. This true story is one of them.

My aunt Ovsanna was the third child in the Varjabedian family of six. She was sixteen years of age and she believed in the life giving promises of the Scriptures and yielded her life to Jesus early in life through her father's influence.

At the start of the First World War, the town criers were advising people to assemble in the town and village centres, leaving all their belongings at home. They were promised that they would be leaving the area for their security for a few days only; then they would come back once the danger was over. The Turkish Gendarmes had alternative plans.

One dark day their worst fears materialised; they were surrounded by armed Turkish Gendarmes, who drove every-body – young men, old men, women and children – to the train station. There they were packed into wagons meant to transport animals and were driven 'as sheep to the slaughter' into the remote dry Syrian desert, an area called Deir-ez-zor.

As the trains were moving through the valley, the rebel 'gendarmes' were shooting down at the passing trains from vantage points in the high mountain chain. My aunt Ovsanna sustained mortal gun shot wounds to the neck and chest; she bled profusely, due to internal haemorrhaging. In a faint voice she asked for a drink of water; alas, where was this water to be found on this train? My mother and grandmother often spoke of Ovsanna's thirst on the train, and how helpless they all felt. Her thirst was so intense, she was getting weaker each passing moment. She somehow knew that she was about to enter into her desired heaven to meet with her Lord and Saviour who would meet her need. So she kept repeating with unquenched lips these words, "I will go and drink of the living water, from the fountain of life in heaven." We believe she was transported by the angels of God into the presence of her Maker and Lord, ever living to welcome us.

Soon her lifeless body was thrown out of the window of the moving train.

The burial of Aunt Ovsanna

I do not wish to omit this paragraph, it is so sacred. After the train had stopped at an unknown destination, my grand-mother, with great sorrow and grief, backtracked countless miles through the desert wilderness, leaving the rest of her young family of three remaining daughters and a baby of six or seven months – her grandson Hagop Junior. He had been orphaned by some unfortunate accident. My uncle, Hagop, the only son and the eldest of the Varjabedian family, had married and had a son called Hagop Junior. I don't know Uncle Hagop's wife's name, but having abandoned her son Hagop Junior she had left for America (I will come to this story later).

My grandmother Mariam walked back for days in the heat, trying to find the spot where her young daughter's body had been slung out of the moving train. Eventually she found the mutilated body and with bare hands she dug a shallow grave, covering Ovsanna's body with earth and stones, and a cross – made with dried twigs! Having comforted her soul, she hastened back along the railtrack, hungry and weary, back to her children.

About my grandmother

Grandmother Mariam, also known as Mariam Bajie ('sister'), spoke Turkish. She had been widowed before the First World War. Her husband had died of an infected, ruptured appendix resulting in peritonitis. Mariam, who had cared for her husband during his illness, worked on a voluntary basis as a nurse while at the same time helping in her cousin's eye clinic. There she learned how to make eye drops, a skill which she put into very good use in her later life, providing for her family by selling bottles of eye drops.

Grandma's testimony

The day Mariam Bajie lost her husband, she prayed to God for additional strength to cope. She was so remarkably helped by God that all the neighbours noticed. When they saw a bonfire in her backyard, they asked her why she was not lamenting the loss of her husband, as was the custom. She replied, "I prayed to God to give me strength from this day on, to be able to care for the lives of the children that God has entrusted into my care. 'To added affliction He adds His grace'." She also quoted Proverbs 3:5-6: "Trust in the LORD with all thine heart; and lean not unto thine own understanding. In all thy ways acknowledge Him, and He shall direct thy paths" (KJV).

The tragedy was not at an end however. Her only son Hagop who had married and had a baby son named Hagop Junior, worked as a guard at a train station. As I have briefly mentioned previously, one day he was hit by an oncoming train and died, leaving behind a loving wife and baby son a few months old.

Rumours of the First World War were in the air. The town criers were sent to village after village to mobilise the public. The Armenian people were told that they would be coming back a few days later and so they should leave all their possessions behind and assemble in the town centre of Hassanbey, or in village squares. Those who stayed at home were forced out. They were crammed into train wagons like sardines. There was such an upheaval no one knew what was happening.

American missionaries rescue orphans

American missionaries came to Armenia to help the plight of orphaned Armenian children. On hearing about the opportunity of transport to America, some women in the area boarded a ship bound for the States. Mariam Bajie's daughter-in-law abandoned her son Hagop Junior, joined the flock of refugees and went to America, never to be traced.

Grandmother voluntarily took on the responsibility of bringing up her grandson. Years later Grandma told us how, in hunger and desperation, she could not find any other way to feed baby Hagop who had been entrusted into her care. Prevailing circumstances were such that she could not provide any sustenance for her family, let alone dried milk for baby Hagop. So she resorted to breastfeeding the baby. By faith she offered her breast to be suckled, and milk flowed. When milk was supplied to her grandson she called this intervention of God a miracle. She breastfed him for two years. Genesis 22:8: "God Himself will provide." Eventually, the family arrived in Beirut, Lebanon, with a donkey, after years of wandering like the Israelites in the deserts of Sinai.

Death of grandson Hagop Junior

Sadly, Hagop Junior's life was cut short at the age of seven. While he was playing in the street, as children do at that age, he was hit by an army truck and killed. Grandmother once again plunged into grief, but she was strong, trusting and leaning on God's promises.

Treating infected eyes

Grandmother was incredibly resilient. In her teenage years she had worked as a voluntary help to one of her cousins who was a renowned ophthalmologist. As I have said, she had been taught how to make eye drops. This was when she lived in Hasan Bey in Turkey.

She made full use of this knowledge. For most of her life she earned a living with this skill, preparing eye drops, filling tiny bottles and selling them to any who came or had been referred to her by an ophthalmologist. Many clients came from near and far to buy these healing eye solutions. She had gained the confidence of the public, because the eye drops had a prompt healing effect on infected eyes. No complications or side effects were ever reported. In short, with the proceeds, she had built a two-storey house in an area called Camp Trad, into which we moved after Dad sold the house he had built. Dad rented the ground floor flat from grandmother and we the grandchildren spent most of our early teenage years in Trad.

2
Early beginnings

My earliest recollections are of the war sirens and the air-raid shelter. One bleak evening with no adults around, we were left in the care of my twelve-year-old sister Naomi. My mother had great confidence in my sister's maternal instinct and her ability to look after us from an early age. It was Naomi's greatest pleasure to have been entrusted by her mother with the care of looking after us.

Naomi had been instructed by our parents to take us down into the air-raid shelter for our safety whenever the siren sounded. I must have been just over a year old and remember this incident very well. On this memorable day the war sirens sounded loud and long. Even though I was so young, I was absorbing the tense atmosphere of danger around me. Our house was so near to the seashore and to the harbour that we could see a warship hit by a bomb. Fire exploded, the surface of the sea was on fire, but instead of being safe in the air-raid shelter, we were gazing at this calamity from our balcony. I was crying in fear and insecurity because I was cold, hungry, and unable to walk down the steps or dress myself. This was the situation, when I noticed how my sister was desperately searching for her Bible, rather than making sure that her baby sister was warmly clothed and carried down to the air-raid shelter. Once she found her Bible she secured it in a cloth bag with string and said, "We can now go down." As we were going down we were aware of further horrific bombs hitting the warship and flames rising from the Mediterranean seashore. We rushed down into the damp dark air-raid shelter, which was already over-crowded.

This incident of my sister's behaviour, looking for her Bible and seeking its protective power instead of securing the lives of her two brothers and little baby sister, left a lasting impression on me. The Bible had been her greatest security, she had put her faith in its words and she had searched for it in the way that someone looks for treasure, something which is valued above all else. That's why it triggered in me a deep spiritual need to find this sacred treasure for myself. My search for God had begun.

Exiled Armenian communities in Beirut

The Armenian exiles that arrived in Lebanon after the First World War formed small communities. Their first and foremost aim was to build churches. There was one well-established Armenian Orthodox Church in Karantina. All Armenian parents were keen to send their children to this well-established Sunday school. We used to love going every Sunday afternoon. It was very noisy, bubbling with the voices of hundreds of children. Nevertheless, through it all, we did learn some truths: "to love our neighbour as ourselves" and "To be good and do well". We sang songs and recited verses learned by heart. Those of us who recited without mistakes were given a beautiful picture and a star for each attendance. I loved going to Sunday school, to find out more about why my sister had spent time during the bombing frantically searching the house for her treasured Bible, rather then leading us to the safety of the air-raid shelter.

The Armenian refugees who had been exiled by the Turks had wasted no time in building schools, as well as churches. There were two schools by this time. One was three miles walking distance, mostly on level roads, the other was further away towards the city centre and was about one hundred feet up on a cliff with very steep steps. These schools were connected to the Armenian Evangelical Church.

Walking down memory lane (pre-school)

Fillor was my close friend who lived across from our house. Her father was entrusted to take care of their rich neighbours' mature orchard during their absence. To keep us off the streets, Fillor's sister would let us play in this garden. She would let us down through a small wooden door by the side of their staircase. We used to spend many happy hours playing houses, hospitals and hide-and-seek. Sometimes we were naughty – and just to mention one instance...

It was Easter time. In most Armenian homes it is customary to prepare for the Easter festival by spring-cleaning. The sitting room gets the best white embroidered linen covers on practically all the furniture. They also all store white wine, with almond sweets, to offer to the well-wishing friends and neighbours, especially for the local Priest when he does his yearly seasonal visits to all his parishioners. Well, one day Fillor's parents were out, so we opened the forbidden secret cupboard where wine and sweets were kept, and guess what? We were tempted to have a taste of the forbidden fruit! To be honest, I can still taste and smell the stolen sip of white wine. This was an experience never repeated as in our home wine had no place, neither for pleasure nor for cooking, there was no spare money for such luxuries. Luckily neither of us got drunk!

Lost and found

On other occasions, whenever I was out of the supervision of a caring sister or mother, I used to love to wander along the seashore. I would keep walking for miles, searching for small shells, bottle tops, anything that I could use to make a pretend dolls house. I would become so involved with this constructive imagination of my childish mind that I would totally lose any sense of time, the need for food or the warmth of home shelter. On more than one occasion my mother, sister and brothers were in every street, calling my name but to no avail. They even got the relatives involved in these searches. One of these searches took many hours and they were at their wits' end by the time I turned up on the doorstep. Unaware of the panic I had caused them, I innocently started showing to them the pearls I had found by the river bank. I had been chasing frogs to bring back home to barbecue. I must have been wet, muddy and smelly, but I was happy and innocent! After all, I had been following my brothers who were with their friends. They were older, yet irresponsible to have left me to wander away on my own. I heard one of my uncles say, "You were lost and now you are found, let us rejoice."

They had to take drastic measures to prevent me getting lost again. I remember being locked in my Aunt Nevart's room. She was widowed and had come to live in one of the rooms which was empty. When she went to work during the week, the whole building was empty. There were no nursery schools to send me to, so they had a brilliant idea to occupy me in aunt's room – they left me with a large bag full of olives to be crushed with a wooden mallet one by one on a square stone. The olives were to be preserved in salt water for winter. To be honest I enjoyed crushing the green olives one at a time. After a few hours I got so tired I fell asleep, so when they arrived they were rather worried, not seeing nor hearing any noise from the room. They were all curiously peeping through the window when I woke up. I was wondering why they were all lined up outside the window looking in. Much as they were pleased to see me alive, I was more than pleased to see them open the door and let me out of the confined space.

Learning obedience and submission

My mother was the main breadwinner. Because of this she was absent most of the time, so naturally we were dependent on our older sister Naomi. My sister had a magical effect on my brothers and me. We feared, respected and obeyed her, and she was loving, caring, strict and, most of all, God fearing. Her only motive was to please God and do the will of God. We were all attached to her, more than we were to Mother or Dad, because they were not always with us. Naomi ran our lives meticulously. She had made a timetable, allocating small tasks to each one of us.

Each morning she would gather us in a circle. We sat on the floor on a piece of rug and she would read a chapter out of her small Gideon Bible (New Testament) and make us each say a short prayer. She would kiss and hug each one of us as she mentioned the tasks she had planned for us to do that day.

I remember being asked to lay the fire for heating the domestic water for our baths. I felt so grown-up being asked to do this task, and to please her I was very busy. We all looked up to her and were good obedient children. Take note, the water had to be collected from the reservoir tap, litre by litre, carried from some distance away and emptied into a ten-gallon petrol tin which was placed on top of three blocks of bricks. I had to start the fire with squashed papers, then add pieces of wood, sit by it and keep putting more wood on the fire, with the rest of the wood piled beside it, and try not to let the fire die out, by using a piece of cardboard to fan it. The water had almost reached boiling point when, all of a sudden, the loose stone prop moved and gallons of boiling water spilled onto my lap, scorching my upper legs. My sister in her panic rubbed the scalded area, and instantly blisters appeared where she had touched. Fortunately old-fashioned remedies seemed to have a fast healing effect, and in a week or two it was completely healed, without leaving any scars.

Twice rescued from drowning

One fine national school holiday, my brothers went to the harbour bridge. I followed them and watched them dive into the sea from a height of 15 feet. I thought I could do the same. I think I was about four years old. I climbed onto a large rock, took off my clothes and down I jumped, hitting my head hard on a rock below the water. Dazed, I went up and down gasping for breath.

By God's grace there were two men some distance away swimming. They must have noticed something unusual, and they came to rescue me. As I was struggling to keep afloat and breathe, one of them grabbed hold of me and pulled me out onto a nearby rock, dangling me head downwards to allow the salt water I had swallowed to drain away from my stomach. This wasn't the last time.

I had not learned my lesson. Another fine sunny day, when we were returning home from school, my brothers asked me to guard their school bags and clothes. I agreed. (You see, the sea and the sand were our playground as we lived very near the seashore.) No sooner had they jumped into the sea than I stripped myself bare and tried to imitate their diving skills. This time it was much more serious as there was no one near by. Somehow one lonely swimmer spotted my disappearance. He must have heard my shouts for help and came to save me from drowning. He was an Arab gentleman, and I am grateful for his swift action. After I had recovered, he gave me a good telling-off and warned me not to dive again.

This remarkable rescue from drowning made me decide not to swim again. Looking back, I see God's angels watching over innocent children and protecting them from harm. Jesus says:

> *"[Satan] comes only to steal and kill and destroy; I have come that they may have life, and have it to the full.'"*
>
> John 10:10

The birth of identical twin girls and their death

There came a period of plenty after the dust of war settled. Dad was once again employed in the harbour canteen, and mother gave birth to identical twin girls. This brought great joy and happiness to the families as a whole.

My sister had started going to school and the rest of us were at home, where we helped mother any way we could. I was so taken up with my baby sisters, I no longer roamed the river banks and the seashore.

During this period Armenia had become one of the 15 Russian Republics. USSR Armenians from the Middle Eastern towns, wishing to emigrate to Armenia as their 'Mother Land', sold their few possessions and enrolled as candidates for emigration. Thousands went to Armenia in 1945. There was such a lot of propaganda; people were promised lands once they got there. Incidentally, though Dad too was encouraged to enrol his family for emigration, our names never came up. This I believe was God's plan for us.

Coming back to the twin baby sisters, they were beautiful, fair-haired, blue-eyed and such healthy bouncing babies that anyone who saw them was thrilled and filled with joy. When they were nine months old Mother took them out for the first time. They were placed opposite each other on a mat in our front yard so that they could crawl around together. After a short time they were brought into the house, to be fed and have their diapers changed. However, in that short time the babies caught an acute infection called Summer Diarrhoea.

Arshaloose died within 40 hours. To save the life of the second twin, Aroosig, Dr Henry Badeer was called. He came right away with bottles of salt-water infusion. 'Clycis' was administered through the abdominal wall, with no result. The infection had weakened the baby, it was not reversible. Aroosig, too, died of dehydration on the ninth day. The happy months were short lived. My mother could not be comforted. Each time we saw her in the kitchen, preparing food, she was singing a lament with tears.

A few years later, when the family moved to Grandmother's house in Trad, Mother gave birth to another baby girl, and this did comfort her for a season. The baby was called Arshaloose because she looked like the first twin. Unfortunately Arshaloose also died of similar symptoms, of acute diarrhoea, a mysterious infection to which there had not yet been found a cure. We all sat around her, prayed and cried. It is very sad to lose another baby, so beautiful and hopeless. I do sincerely believe I shall see them in heaven.

Our first year at school

We were enrolled in the Evangelical school nearest to our home in Karantina, which was about three miles' walking distance. I was in the kindergarten, and my brothers in another class. We walked to and from the school, walking past the military training premises. My sister was enrolled in the school which was further away, a school that was built on a cliff, presumably about one hundred feet high.

One day I was feeling very ill. On this particular day I must have had a high fever. No one knew how bad I was feeling, not even the teachers. After the school was dismissed, my brothers were fooling around together with their friends; they completely forgot me and I lost my way. I was left all on my own, to make my way home from school with hardly any strength in my little legs. I was so ill and sick I could hardly stand. As I lingered on the lonely roads, it got darker and darker. I was disorientated. As I dragged my weary body into the refugee camp by the seashore, all the corrugated cardboard and wooden houses looked like a jigsaw puzzle. I wandered from house to house looking for my mother, but all the faces were strange. By that late evening the rumour of a lost child had spread through the area, but I did not stay with any of the kindly faces. I was determined to find my own way. Eventually, pressing through the maze of huts, I found myself on the main road and shuffled my way home with the help of a kindly lady who seemed to know my mother.

At that young age I thought, if living is as bad as I was feeling that day, I feared I was nearing death. A doctor told my mother that I seemed to be seriously ill with a tummy bug and chest infection. I was feeling a hundred years old. I am glad to say that I have never since had that sort of experience.

Change of school – Armenian Evangelical Central High School

My parents were hard up, unable to provide schooling for four children, so they were advised to move us to another school, which was set on top of a cliff three miles away. There was no public transport so we had to walk to and from school. This school was affiliated to the Armenian Evangelical Church. They had set strict rules. Besides being punctual, honest etc, all the pupils had to attend Sunday school. Those pupils whose parents did not wish to send their son or daughter to a Protestant Sunday school had to send a written statement expressing their reason.

I have mentioned in my previous chapters how much I wanted to find out more about the power and secret protection that the Bible provides, so this principle seemed good to me. I knew I wanted to be at the Sunday school because I would discover more about God. One cold wintry Sunday, my brothers and sister had already gone to Sunday school. I was all geared to go after them, but my mother stopped me because it was raining heavily. It was cold and I had no proper foot-wear. The leather of my wooden clogs had snapped and was hanging by its nail beyond repair. Had it been left to me I would have gone to Sunday school barefoot. I felt I was being pun-ished by my mother and could not understand why I wasn't allowed to go to Sunday school.

On Monday morning, after the morning assembly, the Principal asked all those who had not been to Sunday school to come and stand in front of 400 pupils. I was amongst those who stood in front of the whole assembly. Then we were asked to follow the Principal into his office, and one by one explain why we had been absent. When it was my turn to hold out my hand to be caned, I was so frightened and shy to speak up that I could not express the reason why I had been absent from Sunday school. I received not a few strokes of the cane. It was a bitter medicine to swallow, but I somehow knew it was com-ing from Satan to discourage my faith in God!

In my previous school, in the kindergarten, we had been given French alphabet children's reading books. I was eager to learn and was doing very well; but when I was moved into the new school I was given English alphabet children's read-ing books. I began to confuse the sounds of the letters. I was bewildered, even before being given my own Armenian language alphabet. On top of this, my sister, with every good intention, insisted that I should write with my right hand. She harassed me every time I held a pencil in my left hand. She would slap my hand to make me change and use my right hand. I was born with a genetic left-hand brain centre, but my sister did not know this.

This predicament left me with a stutter and an inferiority complex. I was good at art, arithmetic and embroidery, but I disliked reading and writing. My Armenian lesson teacher was so ignorant that he used to ridicule me in front of a class of 40 pupils. Sometimes it took a whole month before my turn came to read aloud in the class. I hated the teacher, and if it was possible I would dismiss myself from the class, but I used to like the embroidery teacher. Often my classmates would tell the teacher, "Teacher, Ovsanna is using her left hand while embroidering." She would say, "Leave her alone." I used to do my embroidery holding it under the desk.

I was awarded the top prize for embroidery in the whole of the elementary school.

Lost schooling due to illness

During my first year at primary school I was sick with what they called German measles. Because it is an infectious disease I was not allowed back to school for three months and, when I returned to school, I was at a loss, and had great difficulty catching up with the rest of the class, particularly in English lessons. I could never spell a word, and spent hours learning a few lines of a paragraph almost by heart. In the class spelling session, I would muddle the letters in the word. I always got 'zero' as a mark, so much so that my teacher had given up marking my papers, so as not to disappoint me. All the teachers knew I had a certain weakness in reading and writing, but nothing was done to help me, nor was I told what was wrong with me. Only quite recently did I diagnose myself as being dyslexic. Until then I was blaming my sister's good intention, for not letting me use my left hand and being made to use my right hand. My brain could not cope with the change imposed on it and I am still suffering with indecision about which is my right and which is my left, easily losing my sense of direction.

I strongly believe that the interference with my natural ability to use the left side of my body is to be blamed for my not being advanced in speaking five languages, as did most of my classmates at school. Domestic circumstances were also a factor in hindering my advance in school, also frequent change of schools.

Working Saturdays and school holidays

There came a time when my older brother dropped out of school and became the 'bread winner'. From the age of twelve he worked as an apprentice shoemaker. Dad had no regular job. He would do labouring jobs, like tiling kitchen walls and floors, but when the Palestinians came to Beirut, they snatched any work that was going and would do it for much less money. This was one reason for my dad's unemployment; another could have been because he smoked.

He used most of his earnings to buy cigarettes to satisfy his bad habit. The family had to do without some of the basic necessities. Mother did other people's laundry, so that she could buy some food for us. She was very resilient. She knew how to select a certain type of vegetable from the fields around our house and treat it in a special way, which took a few days to prepare. Then she cooked it and provided healthy meals for us and for my cousins. When my cousins called at our house to play, they joined us in eating this very exotic field vegetable dinner. We called it 'panjar'.

We never had birthday parties or gifts at Christmas. We had to buy second-hand school uniforms from those who had grown out of them. Each year in February I used to ask my sister to remind my mother that my birthday was approaching and that I would love to receive a doll for my birthday. However, it was all in vain and my sister would make a rag doll to appease my longing. This is the reason why I love my sister. The rag doll was sufficient to keep me happy, I used to take it to bed to sleep with.

Auntie Vergine had asked my mother if she would allow me to help to clean her flat on Saturday mornings, in order to get some money to buy copy books, pens and pencils, or to be able to buy second-hand school books. We all contributed towards the school fee to top up the scholarship we were receiving from the Armenian Missionary Association of America (AMAA).

Armenian Central High School in Arshefia

The school we attended was called Central High School in Ashrafia. It had a very high standard. As mentioned earlier, pupils had to attend Sunday school. Because of the distance, parents used to bring their children with them to Sunday school and they stayed and attended the church service. School teachers also took Sunday school classes on Sundays. Great importance was given to teaching the Ten Commandments, we were taught biblical truths.

I can only speak for myself when I say that I enjoyed every moment. I used to linger with my friends who lived nearby, to be able to attend the afternoon services, youth groups and Christian Endeavour group. I would often be sent out because I was too young. I loved hearing good preaching, I knew they had found the secret of life in Christ Jesus and I desired to have what they had.

At the same time I was bound with chains of fear, the fear of losing my friends if I became a Christian. Most of them were from well-to-do families; they had money to buy ice cream on Sunday morning, they chewed chewing gum, and spent money on Sundays. As for me, my 13-year-old brother was the breadwinner, I had to beg him to give me money for the Sunday school offering, as well as the fare for the tram to get myself to Ashrafia.

I was in the bad habit of not getting the tram; instead, I would walk to Sunday school. I did not put the offering money into the offering plate, but instead joined my friends in buying ice cream on Sundays – 'keeping up with the Jones?' This I used to love, and found it the most difficult of habits to drop. I was envious of my friends having every luxury, of their pretty dresses, shoes, toys and dolls. I began to develop an inferiority complex, and began to dislike the family I had been born into.

I had many questions to ask God, a 'why me?' complex. In spite of my self-pity, I knew deep within that I was not right with the Lord. He was standing outside my heart, knocking at the door of my heart, but I was not letting Him in one hundred percent. I wanted things to run according to my own plans and desires. I remember arguing with the Lord in my prayer, "I agree with all your teaching, but what's wrong with buying ice cream on Sunday?" The answer came right away, in a still small voice: "You are using the money you should have put into the Sunday school offering." I had to repent and amend my ways. I asked the Lord to forgive me. I believed he forgave me, according to His promises:

> *"If we confess our sins, He is faithful and just and will forgive us our sins and purify us from all unrighteousness."*
> 1 John 1:9

I was more than surprised six weeks later. I was with my friends – they were eating ice cream and chewing gum. I was among them and amused to see them unhappy. I had a peace that passed all understanding. I was on the straight and narrow way which leads to life, and had money saved in my pocket, which was very unusual. The bad habit of buying on Sunday had dropped out of me; without my knowledge God had taken care of it and I didn't have to make any effort.

3

American Lady Visitor

One Sunday morning at Sunday school a visiting lady had come to fill in for an absent teacher. She captured all our attention as she taught us. She spoke to us about salvation in the Lord and we learned the memory verse for that day from Matthew 6:33, "But seek ye first the kingdom of God, and His righteousness; and all these things shall be added unto you" (KJV). She told us the following facts:

"Jesus wishes to come into your hearts, and wants to be friends with you, but you have to prepare your heart for Him to come in. Would you like to put a small stool in your hearts for Him to come in and sit and listen to your prayers, desires, needs? He will meet all your needs, because He loves you and will be faithful to keep his promises to you. All those who would love to obey and welcome Jesus into their heart and lives, please indicate. Who would like to do this?"

She posed this question to the class; naturally we all put our hands up, leaving the pretty American lady satisfied, a duty well done! She taught us Matthew 6:33 by heart. Had it not been for this short and cute story, and the memory verse we learned that day, I would have been tempted to do something stupid! The enemy of our soul is ever trying to devour the children of God. We may be unaware of it at times, but God's Holy Spirit is keenly following us, His children, providing us with a way of escape. "And God is faithful; He will not let you be tempted beyond what you can bear. But when you are tempted, he will also provide a way out so that you can stand up under it" (1 Corinthians 10:13).

Approaching Christmas season and New Year

Approaching the countdown to Christmas triggers unhappiness in me. As a young eight year old, whenever I looked around and considered the circumstances of our home life, I compared them with those of neighbours and friends. I was filled with sadness, anger, jealousy, discontent and a sense of deprivation, partly because my dad was not providing for the family's needs, whereas other fathers were good providers.

Soon after the Second World War, Dad had sold the house in Karantina, with the hope of emigrating to Armenia, but our number never came. The house money was saved in a bank, with the hope of getting interest. However, there was no other income and so within two years it was all spent. The family had to move into Camp Trad region, where Grandmother had built a house a few years earlier. Dad hired the ground floor flat from Grandma for a reasonable price.

Hagop, my older brother, had already left school and started working as an apprentice shoemaker, as I have said, and the rest of us were still at school. Change of home meant even further to walk to attend school.

Poverty was our greatest disadvantage. The wife of a well-to-do relative asked my mother if I could be allowed to help her on Saturday mornings, to clean her house, shake the carpet, sweep the stairs, carry some of her shopping etc. She would give me a meal and pay 50 piasters (equivalent to 50 pence); just enough to buy copy books and pencils. After I had washed the dishes and tidied the kitchen it was time to go home; I was very tired.

The way seemed to get longer and longer, it was a long way home; nevertheless, I used to love working Saturday mornings. I did anything that Aunt Vergine suggested. She had a very kindly face and her voice matched her face. Whenever I did something wrong she would take the blame onto herself and say, "It was my fault," implying she should have explained it more clearly. I used to observe her closely, and because of her tender spirit and wise approach, I was aiming to please her to the best of my ability. I used to polish her dainty ornaments (some were silver and some were brass) until

I could see my reflection in them – so much so that towards the end I would have cramp in my fingers.

One day my mother asked me to go and buy a bunch of parsley from the corner shop. I refused to do the shopping for my mum, simply because she had not asked me in the way that Aunt Vergine used to. I told my mum that I would carry 20 kilograms in weight for Auntie Vergine just because she knew how to ask.

In fact, Auntie Vergine was living a Christ-like life. Throughout the day, she used to write Christian articles for the Christian Endeavour magazine and take nursing school assemblies at the Christian Medical Centre in Beirut. Her husband, Mr Augustine S Badeer, was the hospital administrator (incidentally, my husband is his second cousin). Mrs Vergine Badeer played a great role in my search for Christ. She lived the life and walked the walk. Years later, Aunt Vergine also played a big role in my marriage to John Allen.

Having told you all this, I now return to the countdown to Christmas. On the last Saturday of the year I worked very hard in the morning at my aunt's flat, preparing for their Christmas. She sent me home with a gift of red woollen yarn, enough to knit a sweater (which my sister knitted for me; I wore it for several years, and was grateful for it).

However, all the way home I could see the shop windows decorated with Christmas trees, Santa Clauses, gifts and dolls. I could see more and more decorated shops full of expensive items, a great variety of gifts, including dolls that opened and closed their eyes, all out of our reach to purchase. By the time I arrived home my heart and my emotions were overloaded with sadness and overwhelming self-pity; anger and despair had gripped hold of my mind. As Satan was feeding all sorts of negative thoughts into me I could not face anyone from my family. I got home and hid myself in my grandmother's flat, which was on the first floor – through the balcony door. I sat outside on the balcony crying my heart out, reasoning and worrying with self-pity. The balcony had no protection around it, it was only half finished. The enemy of my soul was once again hard on me. I was looking for a solution to end my misery.

I heard Mum calling me from downstairs, "Ovsanna, come down, the water for your bath is ready." I did not answer her call and she was too busy to come up to console me. I was tired, cold and hungry. As I wallowed in emotional stress, Satan's whispers were getting louder, stronger and stronger. There was a fierce battle taking place in my soul. I cried out loud, "Lord I need your help, please come and help me."

"When I called, you answered me; you made me bold and stout-hearted."

(Psalm 138:3)

It took only a moment; I almost heard an audible voice, like lightning, as clear as a ray of light: "I stand at the door of your heart knocking, invite me in to occupy the small stool you placed in your heart at the Sunday school. Remember, I want to be your closest friend and meet all your desires."

I wish I could explain more clearly. This was the Holy Spirit's voice. It took hold of my cluttered, cloudy emotions and dropped a drop of Jesus' love, dispersing the dark clouds which were over me, replacing them with peace, gladness and joy. I was filled with peace and overwhelming joy, laughing one moment, crying the next. The Holy Spirit continued to whisper, "Jesus is born in your heart, you do not need dolls, which have no life in them. They are only toys, but Jesus is a true living baby born in your heart and soul, who will hear and answer all your needs according to His will." Then the Holy Spirit reminded me of the memory verse (Matthew 6: 33) which we had learned at the Sunday school – "But seek ye first the kingdom of God, and His righteousness; and all these things shall be added unto you" (KJV).

(Incidentally, Armenians celebrate Christmas on the sixth of January.)

As an eight-year-old child I had difficulty in understanding the meaning of the word 'righteous'. I looked it up in the dictionary and found the following adjectives – 'just; upright;

godly; virtuous; good; honest', and when I read the verses before Matthew 6:33 (chapter 6, verses 30 to 32) they condemned me for worrying: "O you of little faith". Verse 32 calls those who worry about what we eat and wear as pagan. Our Heavenly Father knows that we have need of them. (Once I was blind but now I see.)

I ran down the steps, hugged my mum and said, "Jesus is born in my heart." I had been born again. I invited Him into my heart, He has come to stay and live in my heart, and He is in control of my life from now on. Jesus said, "Unless you change and become like little children, you will never enter the kingdom of heaven" (Matthew 18:3).

I was now a born-again believer. My mother was pleasantly surprised and was glad that she had not come up the steps to counsel me. I had my bath, ate my supper, helped Mum to prepare the food for Sunday, and encouraged her to go to church with me. In the morning we both went to church. She used to love attending, but due to household chores she missed going. Armenian meals take a long time to prepare, and in those days there was no such thing as instant food. I am glad to say that a few weeks later she too came to the Lord and gave her heart to Him.

She had a small tiny hymn book, which had Turkish words written in Armenian lettering. It had the same tunes as the Methodist hymns. The only English words she knew were John 3:16 – "God so loved the world that He gave His one and only Son, that whoever believes in Him shall not perish but have eternal life." She had learned this verse from the British missionaries early in her childhood days.

In her last four years she lived with my sister in Montreal, Canada. She died there in 1993 – all her four children and 16 grandchildren were present. She was 84 years old. $1,000 was donated to the first Armenian Church in Montreal by the people who knew her and the church family members.

My new life in Jesus

I had fallen in love with Jesus, had found a new life as the Bible says: "If anyone is in Christ, he is a new creation;

old has gone, the new has come!" (2 Corinthians 5:17). I could now see life in a way that Christless eyes can never see! I was now so enthusiastic. My mission was to let others know – proclaim what He has done for my soul.

Heaven's answer to earth's problems is to go another way. Like the three wise men did, in Matthew 2:12, I changed my way, and followed the star.

[Jesus said], "I am the way and the truth and the life."
(John 14:6)

I was full of songs; I had a little harmonica (mouth organ) and used to take it with me everywhere and play choruses. I used to walk up the hills around our house, sit under the pine trees and sing all on my own, spending time with the Lord and praying.

I longed to stay in His presence, had a deep hunger to get to know Him more. I was given a Gideon New Testament in my own Armenian language. I loved reading it; it was my only possession and I used to carry it with me and read it as often as I could. One day I lost it and looked everywhere but could not find it. I prayed, "Lord, whoever finds it or has stolen it, may he or she become a Christian." God is not anyone's debtor. Aunt Persap Bedeer gave me another New Testament, which I still have and use.

At the weekends I visited my friends and told them how I had become a born-again Christian. When I saw friends in the street I testified to them. I wished that all would repent and follow Jesus' Commandment to love one another. Jesus said, "Unless you change and become like little children, you will never enter the kingdom of heaven."

God's love was changing me. It has never stopped doing so. It gets harder and at the same time gets better. By this I mean the Holy Spirit moulds us like clay in the Master Potter's hand, until He has a vessel fit for the Master's use. Mind you, in the process He uses no anaesthetics or painkiller, but He is still a gentle God.

Home life

My mother's life had been a string of hardships, which she used to grin and bear. She never complained, but focused on achieving her best in the given circumstances. She had had no opportunity to go to school. She and her sisters survived the Armenian 'Holocaust'. All that she had seen and heard from a devoted mother, she put into practice. She was hard working, honest, kind, hospitable, generous and devoted to her children. Her husband had left her with all the responsibility of caring for the children.

> *The wife of noble character:*
> *"She is worth far more than rubies. Her husband has full confidence in her."*
>
> (Proverbs 31:10-11)

As mentioned before, it was hard for Dad to find a job. When the French army was in Beirut, he was employed as kitchen staff. Then the army sent him to Tel Aviv to work for a season. On his way back home, bandits robbed him. They robbed him of all his documents and left him as dead. On his arrival home he was weak, unable to find work, and whenever he did find work it would be for only a few days a week. He gave some of what little he earned to Mother and with the rest he would buy cigarettes. This bad habit of Dad's ruined our family life and joy.

We never had enough for gifts, birthday celebrations or even a Christmas tree or turkey. At this period in my life, I too had a bad habit of spending money on unnecessary things. With the Sunday school collection money I used to buy lipstick and hairpins to glamorise myself. One day Dad got angry with me when he saw what I was using the money for, and said, "Your sister is ten years older then you and yet she does not spend money as you do for such cosmetics." That was a stern warning. I stopped that bad habit, because Dad did not approve. Furthermore I realised that such things, small as they may seem, may grow into a big expensive trap – you fall in and are unable to pull yourself out; so best to shake it off.

A puny attempt to challenge my dad

Here is another incident. On a bright sunny Sunday I arrived home from an exciting Sunday school session and found my dad at home on his own, smoking. Dad was never allowed to smoke in the house, because mother could never stand the smell of cigarette smoke, so Dad used to put the cigarette out before coming into the house. I very innocently said, "Dad, if you only hearken to your youngest daughter and give up smoking, you will go to heaven." How I touched his most sensitive nerve!

Dad was not expecting such a challenge from his youngest child. He got very angry and hit my face with the back of his hand. With the force of his punch the wedding ring on his right hand caught my nose, which started bleeding profusely. At the time I was standing behind the kitchen door; I hung my head to avoid soiling my dress; I did not even dare to cry because I was hurting deeply – it felt as though there was a huge lump in my throat. Dad did not only strike me, he also abused me with words, using the Turkish language which I understood. That hurt me all the more and I made up my mind never ever to speak to Dad about eternal truths again.

A few minutes later Mother arrived from shopping. She just saw the pool of blood on the kitchen floor and was flabbergasted. Trembling from head to toe I had to assure her that I was all right. "'My thoughts are not your thoughts, neither are your ways my ways,' declares the LORD" (Isaiah 55:8).

For 27 years all those who knew my dad made silent prayers. The prayers were answered. Read on; do not miss this episode. I will come to it later.

Blind friend Neuvart Keucheukian

While in Trad, my brother Bedros and I attended a local school, only a short walking distance from home. English missionaries who spoke fluent Armenian had newly set up this school. They also erected special safe buildings for the blind, working facilities for the unemployed men and homes for needy families and for those who had been widowed.

The junior school was opposite the blind school. Pupils were given permission to befriend the blind students. I made friends with an ugly looking blind lady called Neuvart. She had a limp. Not many would have taken to her, but she had a heart of gold! I was not shy to befriend her and took her by the hand to Sunday school, to church and sometimes to my home. Our walks together were like Luke 24:13-15, where two men are walking to a village called Emmaus, and Jesus joins them.

Neuvart was a good knitter. To keep me warm she knitted two woollen cardigans for me before I left Beirut to come to England. She also embroidered two most beautiful lace tray covers as leaving presents. We kept in touch for many years, she was God's gift to me. I miss her very much.

The blind school choir were singing one evening. I was at the school drama practice and heard them sing. I truly believed there were angels singing in the sky. I felt uplifted and worshipped with them – it was so soothing to hear them sing.

I saw an Unidentified Flying Object

In the school in Trad, around 1946-7, while all the pupils were in the classroom, I was sitting at my desk, nearest to the door. I suddenly heard a great crashing noise; I thought the buildings were crashing; I ran out of the classroom to see what it was that I had heard. To my great astonishment, I saw this strange flying object. It looked like a grey, circular, swerving object. Whether it was concave or convex was not so clear to my eyes. It had passed so very swiftly, like a flash of lightning; within a few seconds it had disappeared, high up on the horizon. I shall never forget the sight. I began to wonder what it could have been. Certainly it did not look like an aeroplane. I did ask questions about this strange flying object. Years later, I heard people talking of seeing an object similar to the one I have just described; they called it a UFO.

Death through Tetanus infection

Another remarkable incident took place, which could have been avoided.

Garo, my friend, was a young boy with whom I shared a

desk in the class. One Friday afternoon, as he was playing on the school playing field, his little toe got punctured with a piece of barbed wire fencing from around the school playground. Soon after he reported it he received treatment. The punctured wound did not bleed. I was at the scene. It required little skill to clean the wound with Iodine wipes and dress it with Band-Aid. Being the weekend, the school was dismissed and we all went home. Garo's mother had to go to work the whole of Saturday and Sunday, leaving him at home unattended.

On Monday morning Garo made his way to school, not feeling well at all. He kept saying to the teacher, "Look teacher, I can't open my mouth." He said it over and over by putting his index finger and thumb into his mouth. "I can't open my mouth any more." The teacher, unaware of the symptoms of lockjaw (tetanus), did nothing about it, so the poor boy spent all that day in school with a very high fever. On Monday evening his mother realised that her son was delirious with a high temperature. She called the hospital and he was transferred to intensive care. Within 20 hours he died. It was too late, and so sad to lose a friend so young. It could have been avoided.

All the school attended Garo's funeral. I trust the teachers of today may not make the same mistake.

My brother Bedsos and I spent a year in this local school in Trad. Naomi graduated from high school in the same year.

A year in village school

Soon after her graduation my sister Naomi was asked to take a teaching post at an Armenian primary school in a village called Zahle. It was two hours' drive by car, right up beyond the Lebanon mountain range.

The climate up there in Zahle is much cooler, and it snows most of the winter months. It was decided that I should accompany her, so we both spent a happy year together in this remarkable village school. I was still only around nine years old.

Zahle was one of the best-known holiday centres. The village valley is renowned for its river bank walks, cafeterias, coffee shops, gift shops, cabarets, restaurants and casinos. A mini Las Vegas. The river surface used to freeze in the midwinter chill. Whenever the school closed, because of the freezing temperatures, some naughty children would be tempted to walk or fool around on the frozen riverbank, endangering themselves. This was prohibited and after a few accidents the security police would guard the area.

Reverend Avakian was the principal of the school (he was related to my mother). Pupils were all allocated small tasks. Mine was to light six charcoal portable stoves, one for each classroom, and occasionally to clear the snow on the school steps.

One cold school day, having fulfilled my duties and on hearing the school assembly bell, I hurried up the steps and got into my line. While the principal was announcing some activities, I was losing consciousness. I felt as though I was going down and down into a dark tunnel. I fell on the pupil standing behind me. She pushed me and I fell on the person in front of me. She raised the alarm that I had fainted. The principal must have slapped my face for a considerable number of times to rouse me. I began to hear a faint sound, as though coming from distant horizons. It got louder and louder, nearer and nearer. Then I heard my name and eventually I regained consciousness. Later the principal assumed I might be anaemic and he suggested that I should eat more green vegetables.

On the whole it was an enjoyable year with a difference. Once the year's teaching contract was completed, we returned home to the Trad district of Beirut, Lebanon. We were sad to leave the friends we had made.

I spent one more year in Trad school. Moving back to Central High School (CHS) in Ashrafia, Bedros dropped out of school, tried several jobs and eventually settled with a gentleman tailor who knew how to handle him, and he became a tailor. Hagop became the breadwinner. Dad did not have a permanent job.

Palestinians, driven out of Palestine, had almost invaded Lebanon, chasing all the jobs they could find. They were paid much less money, so Dad could not find jobs that he could do.

I attended one more year at the local school. Then I went

back to CHS and got enrolled on the scholarship list. I too had to work to top up the school fees. To do this, I became a baby-minder during the summer holidays. Money never touched my hand; the parents of the child I cared for gave the money to the school secretary at the start of the school year.

The CHS had one of the best academic records. In addition it had very high moral standards and was very strong on discipline.

The school day started at 7.30am. Five classes were held in the morning and three sessions in the afternoon. Four language lessons were compulsory. I was always behind in my lessons due to a dyslexic tendency, but good in maths, drawing, drama, embroidery and art. At the end of my elementary year graduation, I was awarded three trophies for punctuality, good behavioural character and best embroidery. I shall never forget. At the graduation, on the pulpit, there was a large prize. I was wondering whose it was going to be. When my name was read out, I thought the Principal had made a mistake and looked for another person to be called. They all indicated that it was for me. I went up to the platform four times, including receiving the diploma. It really was dazzling to hear all the clapping and encouragement the parents and teachers showed, beyond my belief. I wondered if they knew something different! I had quite an inferiority complex.

An inferiority complex is something Satan offers and we accept, not knowing where it is coming from. But when God looks at His children, He sees not as Satan does, but God sees us through the shed blood of Jesus, and condemns us not. Just think of it, how it feels to be accepted by His beloved son Jesus.

A wedding and a funeral

It was my sister's wedding day. That morning I had been asked to do a number of unfinished tasks. There were some invitations waiting to be delivered, which had not yet been given out. Some of the invitations were to be by word of mouth, of course. Other last minute preparations had to be rounded up, such as flowers brought in and the church decorated.

On arriving at the church I found the lower Iron Gate barred. I had no idea why and I had to squeeze in through the side entrance door into the yard. To my horror I was confronted with a peculiar smell of burnt flesh and petrol. The ceiling of the entrance lobby looked discoloured with soot. I stood perplexed, wondering what had happened.

The church's caretaker and family lived within the church grounds. Alice, the youngest daughter of the caretaker, had been my classmate, and the eldest daughter, Armenoohie had been my sister's classmate. They had graduated together. Armenoohie got married, while my sister had taken up nursing.

Armenoohie had two small sons within three years of her marriage and lived not too far from her own family. We all thought that she was coping well as a mother. When she had been at school she was always top of her class, year after year, no one could match her ability at school work. But for some unknown reason, Armenoohie had been put into a psychiatric hospital for appropriate treatment to relieve her stressful home situation. After a period of hospitalisation, she had been sent home to her parents to recuperate from her illness (postnatal depression).

As I stood wondering, my friend Alice came over with a grim face to impart the very sad news of her older sister Armenoohie's death.

Armenoohie had got up very early that morning and set herself on fire, having poured petrol on herself, lit a candle and burnt herself outside their kitchen door. Her father had smelled the burning, come out and to his horror found his daughter engulfed in flames. With his bare hands he had tried his utmost to put out the flames. But he only burned his hands. She had been transferred to hospital but had died in the ambulance.

Can you imagine how I felt? I looked for the minister, who also lived in the church residence, to find out if the wedding was still to take place. I was told, "Yes."

There were only a few of us who knew about this calamity. We had to keep it a secret until the wedding was over. I was also told that the funeral was to take place after the wedding on the very same day, in the afternoon. This was because it was Saturday, and on Sunday there was to be a church service in the same hall, while on Monday school would start in earnest.

I had to go back home to change into my bridesmaid's outfit. The wedding took place as planned at one o'clock; the wedding march played, the hall filled with friends, relatives, neighbours and the church/school community. It was an Armenian wedding which everyone is free to attend, whether invited or not. They are given small tokens of sugar almonds to take home.

I took my place in the front row near the altar, holding a bunch of flowers. I was so tired, hungry and sorrowful, I could no longer stand up, and fainted. Fortunately, my class teacher was sitting next to me and she helped me to regain my composure.

At the reception the news of the death of Naomi's best friend was made known to her. There was a mixture of emotions and questions. Why should such things take place in life? But one day it shall all be revealed.

This dear family, who had lost their very dear daughter, leaving behind two little sons bereft of their mother, did find solace in God alone.

> *"And we know that in all things God works for the good of those who love Him, who have been called according to His purpose."*
>
> (Romans 8:28)

School visit of Miss Helen Keller

The school administrator had planned and organised the visit of Miss Helen Keller. This remarkable lady had overcome her blindness and deafness, achieved the highest academic degrees and become famous, with the help of her teacher who had discovered the touch method of communication. Helen Keller had read the history of the Armenian nation's plight and faith. She desired to get to know more about this nation and to help and encourage the Armenian parents to give their children a good education.

The event was well publicised. The tickets were highly priced and sold; without a ticket no one could have access to the auditorium. The students were given a day off. Government officials, religious heads, teachers, people in authority, police – they were all expected to stand in a queue to welcome this distinguished, renowned lady, Helen Keller.

I didn't want to miss this great opportunity of seeing Miss Helen Keller. So I offered to help the school caretaker with the preparation. All the classrooms had to be cleaned, the large hall floor to be scrubbed, washed and dried, the windows and toilets cleaned; everything had to look clean and perfect. Extra chairs were brought in. My friend and I worked hard, together with members of the caretaker's family. We did all that we were told to do. We both helped, in order to see and hear Miss Helen Keller's life story, to hear how she had achieved impossible heights in spite of her infirmity. It defies human reasoning what she had managed to achieve during her lifetime.

When the time arrived, as the dignitaries were gathering, we made our way to a vantage point from which we could see and hear and not miss anything.

Miss Helen Keller appealed to the congregation to help educate their children. She offered a large sum of money towards Armenian schools; this was followed by a rich businessman's offer, and another large amount by cheque. It kept snowballing and at the end they announced the total sum promised.

As for me, I was challenged. I learned never to give up. Obstacles are the stepping stones to advancement.

Visit of a young preacher

Samuel Doctorian came to speak at the Central High School assembly. He was 17 years old, a young preacher full of the Holy Spirit, boldly declaring the love of Jesus. He said that Jesus had laid down His life for each and every one of us, that our unrighteous acts were laid on Him, that He had been crucified in our place, to give us salvation; that He bore our penalty of sin on His body by being crucified in our place, in exchange for life eternal.

While he was 15 years old, working as a shoemaker in a dark attic room, Samuel had heard God's voice calling him, "Samuel, Samuel, leave everything and follow me, and I will make you a fisher of men."

From the age of five Samuel had wished to be a preacher of the Word of God; this voice was so clear he had no doubt whatsoever that God was calling him to serve Him.

In a short time he told the pupils about his visit to Africa, where he had seen leprous people, shaken hands with them and spoken to them about the love of Jesus. There was a great response from them. This was the moment that I heard the still, small voice say, "Who will go for me?" My innermost being said, "I will go." Where no one has ever gone before, I will care for the needy and the leprous people. This was the moment I made up my mind to become a nurse, and then go to whichever mission the Lord would appoint for me.

After school, I used to take the longer road to the Christian Medical Centre Hospital, just to observe the nurses in their green nursing uniforms. I thought nurses were angels and I admired them. One such day, I noticed a bloodstained sheet hanging in the washroom. I thought, how disgusting to hang such a dirty sheet near an open window, what must the passers-by think of the Christian Medical Centre, where my sister had started working as a nurse.

I thought to myself, "When I become a nurse, I will make sure such dirty sheets are not seen from outside, and I will make sure everything looks clean and well placed."

However, at school I was not performing well. I could not study all the subjects and when I arrived home I could concentrate on one or two subjects only. Those which were difficult were left unprepared, because Dad wanted the light to be turned off in the evening and in the morning we had to get up very early to get ready for school. It was suggested that it would be best if I left school a year early and started to study nursing. So I applied for a nursing course and was accepted.

4

The first Armenian Hospital in Beirut

As mentioned in earlier chapters, Armenian exiles from Turkish towns and villages had made their way to Beirut in Lebanon. But those who had fled to the neighbouring countries did not dare to return to the mercy of the Turks.

The Armenian deportee leaders asked the French authorities for protection and safe passage out of Turkey. The French Government put them on French boats and sent them to Cyprus, but they were refused permission to land. Then they went to Egypt and Greece, where only a few selected people were given asylum. After that, boats took them to Izmir, a town in Turkey; but the Armenians refused to disembark in Turkey so, in desperation, the French boats brought them to the shores of Lebanon, which was a French mandate. Here they were forced to disembark and the boats left.

The Armenian refugees built huts with corrugated iron to be protected from the cold and rain.

There were many thousands of homeless and penniless Armenians who landed in Lebanon. After nearly 20 years of struggles, great numbers made their homes in Beirut. Being an industrious people, they found work to provide bread for their children. Some eventually started small businesses, and all of them moved from the seashore to Camps along the Beirut river regions.

Two young Christian doctors, Dr Puzant Krikorian and Dr Peter Manoogian, fully aware of the need and the plight of their Armenian countrymen, wanted to set up a medical centre where they could give good medical care to the poor, at a rate they could afford. They also wanted to serve their Lord and provide a Christian atmosphere with the medical care.

They realised the magnitude of such an undertaking and their inability to carry out the business negotiations, so they asked Mr Augustine S Badeer, a fine Christian businessman, to join them; to him fell the burden of hunting for a proper location.

A piece of land on a steep hill was found. These three men gave all they had, and their dream and aspirations began to materialise. They named the hospital the Christian Medical Centre (CMC).

The hospital was dedicated on 1 January 1948.

In October 1949 the nursing school was set up by Miss Iola McClellan, a Baptist missionary nurse, who was asked to set the curriculum and do the teaching. Five students were registered in the first year class. One of them was my sister. In 1952 they were the first graduates.

Entering the nursing school was my greatest ambition. As soon as the school year was over I presented myself to the nursing Matron, Miss Margaret Blanchard. The light green nurses' uniform was already waiting to be worn – I had already made it myself at home.

I followed in my sister's footsteps in 1955. By this time the hospital was in its sixth year – numbers of staff and patients growing. Dr Manoogian and Dr Krikorian held clinics daily. They were skilled surgeons and had both gained their experience working with Dr Harry R Bayes from Kennedy Memorial Hospital in Tripoli.

In my class there were six students to begin with but two dropped out during the first term. We worked nine-hour shifts. Our tutors were from Switzerland, Miss M Blanchard, Miss Zulauf and Miss Eymann. A number of doctors assumed responsibility for the medical subjects.

Our day started at 7.30am. After serving breakfast to the patients we all went down to daily services in the chapel. Classes began right after chapel, soon after 8am. One or even two classes were conducted at a time, while some of the nurses had to care for the work in the clinic and on the hospital floors. Sometimes there was only half-an-hour's break for lunch before the afternoon classes.

"Study to show thyself approved unto God" (2 Timothy 2:15, KJV) has been the motto of the students since the CMC Hospital School of Nursing began on 16 October 1949.

Another great day in the life of each student is the day she receives her cap! It is always an impressive service when the nurses light their lamps and are challenged to pattern their life of service after the great 'Lady of the Lamp' Florence Nightingale. At the capping services they are told that the word 'CAP' stood for a Christ-like Appearance to People; as they served the people, they were to do so with the spirit of Christ.

The nursing school curriculum was a three-year course. The students received instruction and experience in the specialities hospitals such as: mental and nervous diseases, in Asfourieh for psychiatry and Azounier Sanitorium for tuberculosis nursing and other chest ailments and for surgery. Miss A Zulauf taught paediatrics.

The course looked long and hard and I felt very insufficient as my knowledge of English was limited. The Armenian-English dictionary was much in use. I remember studying until 4am. Once, Doctor Krikorian returned from a church committee meeting at around 4am and thought the lights had been left on. When he came to turn them off, he found me in the classroom studying in the early hours of the morning. He advised me to leave and go to bed.

Some highlights during nursing school at the CMC Hospital

The earthquake tremor

One day, after I had finished working with the patients, I came back to the nurses' dormitory, had a shower, did some studying, went and lay on my bed and soon fell asleep. A few minutes later I felt my bed shaking. I opened my eyes and asked out loud who was disturbing me.

My room-mates all looked at me with surprise and said, "None of us are guilty, we are all shaking; it's an earthquake."

I thought, 'Well, I have made my peace with the Lord.' Strangely enough, there was such peace in my heart, I felt philosophical. I got up, went to the roof of the hospital, and looked down on to the road below. To my amazement, I saw a pregnant lady who was expecting twins, hurrying towards the safety of the hospital. Seeing her I remembered the passage in the Scripture, Matthew 24:19, "How dreadful it will be in those days for pregnant women and nursing mothers!"

It is truly frightening when the earth on which you stand becomes unstable. This earthquake incident reminded me of our spiritual state, when sudden difficulties hit us in our lifetime, as suggested in the hymn which we often sang at the Christian Youth gatherings, 'Will your anchor hold, when the billows roll?'

A patient walks out of the window

A middle-aged patient was admitted to a private room in the hospital. He was tall and hefty and had been an alcoholic for many years. It was my responsibility to take care of him during the daytime. I must admit it was quite difficult to please him. He spoke non-stop and in such a persuasive way about the things he heard and saw. In actual fact he was hallucinating constantly. I had to sit by him, and reassure him that there were no rats under his bed and that the dogs were not barking at him. It was a huge relief to go off duty after being with him for several hours. The following morning all the nurses were round the desk to receive the night nurse's report. I was shaken to hear the night nurse telling us that the middle-aged man had walked out of the window in pursuit of those rats.

He had fallen from the second-storey department approximately 20 feet in height. The senior doctor, whose bedroom was next to where the patient had fallen in the early hours of the morning, heard the groans and moans. He thought there must have been a thief by his window trying to get into his flat. The doctor called his colleague, and with torches they went behind the hospital wall and the wooden fence. They struggled to reach the patient, lifted him into a wheel chair and carried him back into his bed. Fortunately he had no broken bones, only some scratches and bruising.

The hospital had no insurance policy as yet at the time.

The doctors counted their blessings, because the patient had come out of this incident very lightly; he had survived the fall. I believe that, by the grace of God and the protection of our morning prayers, there was an umbrella of divine protection over every activity. Faith and trust in the Lord are the best insurance you can ever have.

Night-nursing

I found night-nursing very difficult. I could not sleep during the day because of the heat and noise. The hospital launderette was on the roof, opposite the night nurses' dormitory. The ladies who worked at the launderette wore clogs. The roof used to shake as they walked, they talked in loud voices, and on top of this, the flies and mosquitoes were enough to keep me awake.

One day, after struggling to sleep, I was just about falling to sleep when there was a knock at the door. A friend from the newly-established Bible school woke me up; she had come to take me with her to go into the room of a dying man to talk about Jesus.

I was in no mood to go down, to evangelise to a dying man. I plainly told her, "Sorry, you can go on your own and tell him what the Lord has put in your heart." After she left my room I had some soul-searching to do. I began to blame myself for not joining her, and this feeling of self-condemnation carried on for several months. I felt I had disobeyed the Holy Spirit's prompting of my friend. Would the Lord forgive me for such bad behaviour? I needed to repent and get back my peace. I learned a vital lesson: 'to put others before myself'.

My brother's wedding

My brother Bedros' wedding day was nearing. I had spent my money on his new house and realised I had no suitable dress to wear for the wedding. I prayed and decided that I would make an excuse and not attend the wedding.

One of my patients, whom I had nursed a couple of months previously, had died. She had left me 25 Lebanese pounds in her will. This strange man came to the hospital looking for me and trying to give me an envelope. He said, "This is from Mrs Kasargian; you nursed her two months ago, she has left this legacy for you."

I was in a bit of trouble. We were not allowed to accept gifts or tips from the patients. I pleaded with this gentleman, "Sorry, we are not allowed to accept gifts, because it's the hospital's rule."

He insisted, "This is a legacy, you do not refuse legacies." So I finally accepted the legacy in a brown envelope from him.

After he left, as I was pondering, I realised it was the Lord's way of meeting my needs. I went and bought some yellow woollen material, which I took to the dressmaker. I told her how the money had come and she made a beautiful dress. When I wore it at the wedding I felt like a princess.

The revival in town (by Reverend Samuel Doctorian)
The town of Beirut was echoing with songs of revival. We, the nurses, could hear the songs echoing from the distant valley beyond the river below the hospital building. From the balcony of the hospital, we watched lorries full of children, men and women making their way to the tent meetings. We were not allowed to leave the hospital; we could only go home when we had a day off.

Once I was on duty I used to dedicate myself completely to looking after the patients; I never wasted any time. The matron used to chase me to send me to my lunch, otherwise I would forget that it was lunch hour.

It was compulsory to study two hours every night in the classroom from 7 to 9pm. This was disastrous as each student began to tell the funny side of things that had happened at hospital bedsides. Some hilarious jokes were told. One nurse was particularly good at telling us stories in a humorous way. In the end this nurse failed her lessons and was not able to carry on disturbing the rest of the students; she was sent home. After that, the tutors decided to take turns to watch over us in the classroom during study period.

One day I had worked all day and it was my day off the following day. However, I had totally forgotten that the next day was my day off. I received a telephone call from a friend with whom I had worked in the sanatorium. She asked me if we could go together to a Revival meeting to be held in a tent especially set up in the town's largest football field. The telephone triggered my memory, then one of the staff nurses coming down from the hospital floor was surprised to see me in the hospital. She said, "Oh, what are you doing here? You have a day off tomorrow, you should be at home." On hearing this I left to go home.

I was so glad I could go to the tent meeting with my friend. I knocked at the study room door and, very excited, said to the teacher, "I am going." Sister tutor was there to monitor the study session. The sister had forgotten that it was my day off, so she went and complained to the manager that I had excused myself from the study session without prior permission. In fact, I had excused myself on the grounds of 'having a day off the following day'.

A day after, when I returned on duty, I was called to the manager's office and was told that I had broken hospital rules. I was told to go and take off my cap, and work without it for a month. Without my cap, for a whole month! I was stunned, I did not deserve such a degradation. I was shocked, could not say a word and felt that I had been made a scapegoat.

From then on I worked so very hard and with a brave face did the most menial jobs, such as cleaning the bedpans and toilets, scrubbing the walls and windows etc. Then I went to the chapel and cried my heart out.

When I met my sister's sister-in-law, Alice Albarian, I shared my depression with her. Sister Alice was my Sunday school teacher. She said that if I was in Christ Jesus, these arrows that had been thrown at me were from Satan, I should not allow them to affect me. If I considered myself as 'dead in Christ', then the arrows should bounce back. I had to put on Christ, and hide in Him.

"Integrity always wins and builds character"
Two weeks later everyone in the hospital noticed how cheerfully I was working under the circumstances. The worst thing

was when the patients asked me where my cap was. I said that I had been told I had broken the hospital rules. At the end of the second week, I was called into the office and Mr Badeer said that they had seen me work with such humility and integrity I could go and put my cap back on. Even at this interview with Mr Badeer, I was not allowed to explain the situation, how I had been misunderstood and misjudged.

However, the tent meeting was one I shall never forget. God's presence was in evidence. Rev Samuel Doctorian felt in his spirit that a few naughty hooligans had come to interrupt the meeting, so, in the middle of his prayer, he prophesied, "There are some men who have come to disturb the presence of the Lord; the Spirit is going to strike and they will be carried out on stretchers by four men. Please, Lord, spare their lives and their souls," he pleaded. Behold, these men fell on to the ground and were carried out by four men.

The news of this event spread throughout the town. Many came to seek the Lord. Every night trucks full of children, men and women attended the tent meetings that lasted three weeks. Because of my nursing job I had to stay within the hospital. We used to hear the people going to these meetings rejoicing and singing choruses in three languages. The town was vibrant with people singing. My brothers also came and accepted the Lord as their Saviour. At home the conversation was all about the wonderful things that were taking place.

The revival meetings continued after the tent was removed at the end of three weeks. The small churches in the region held Gospel meetings and testimonies were heard. The one nearest to us was at the Tatickian school hall. I attended a few evenings and was greatly blessed with what I heard, learned and saw.

When the appeal was given, people were very generous in giving; they knew they were giving to a good cause. I had been given a gold cross with a chain, which had belonged to my sister. Here is how she obtained this gold. After her high school graduation, she had worked in a dental surgery. (People used to have gold fillings or gold teeth made at the dental clinics.) When the clients were asked to rinse out their mouths, the mouthwash solution passed through a pipe down into a bowl with a sifting net. The gold fragments used to accumulate in the filter bowl. At the end of each day, she had to clean and discard the rubbish. She was told, "You could save the gold fragments for yourself." After a year of saving, she had quite a substantial amount of gold bits. Mother knew a goldsmith who was skilful in crafting gold crosses and chains, so she took the gold bits to him and he formed a beautiful heavy gold necklace.

The same year, my sister decided to change her job. She wished to go back to general nursing, rather then dental nursing. She applied to the Katar Oil Company Hospital in the Arabian Gulf State of Kuwait for a position as staff nurse. She was ready to leave. A smart Christian gentleman, Mr Haroutun, had his eye on her and asked if they could get engaged before she left for her new job in Katar Hospital.

At the engagement ceremony it is customary for the bridegroom to give a gift in gold to the bride-to-be. Haroutun presented her with a beautiful gold cross on a chain, and so Naomi gave her own gold cross to me. I only wore it once.

When the appeal for the continuation of the Gospel meetings was announced, ladies were taking off their jewellery and placing everything in the offering plate. The ushers were making sure all was collected. Many who had money gave money, but I had no other possessions, just the new cross and chain, a gift from my sister. I obeyed the inner voice, called the usher to the side room and said, "The Lord told me to give this cross to the work of the Lord, so that His kingdom be extended in this earth, so that many would hear His call to get to know God." The usher asked, "Does your mother know what you are doing?" I said, "No, but the Lord knows." He took the cross and chain. It was like the widow's mite. "But she, out of her poverty, put in everything – all she had to live on" (Mark 12:44). Jesus referred to it in his talk of appreciation. I had given the cross and chain gladly and willingly, and forgot about it for many years. Strangely enough, neither my mother nor my sister ever asked me about it. It was taken care of by God.

Many years later, in Matlock in England where I live at

present, Mrs J Potter, the pastor's wife, and her friend came to visit me. The friend suddenly blurted out the words, "You are lucky, living in such surroundings." When I heard the word 'lucky', I felt a righteous indignation. At that moment, for the first time, I remembered the gold cross, and thought that it was not luck but the promise of the Scriptures: "Give, and it will be given to you. A good measure, pressed down, shaken together and running over, will be poured into your lap. For with the measure you use, it will be measured to you" (Luke 6:38). This was exactly a reward from God. I wanted God to have the glory. I had come to this house with one suitcase. "Seek first His kingdom and His righteousness, and all these things will be given to you" (Matthew 6:33).

5

Ambition to serve the Lord

After the revival, a Bible school was set up and twelve students were enrolled. Three years later these twelve graduated. The Bible school continued and I was looking forward to joining them after my graduation and becoming a Bible woman or missionary. This was my vocation and calling, to go where He led me. I spent my two weeks of annual leave as a camp nurse with needy children at the Kechag summer retreat. I worked together with others in Kechag camp, near Beit-Mari village, where 150 undernourished children from poorer families had been nominated as suitable candidates for three weeks of fresh air, good food, sports and games, mingled with Christian ethics. Children aged from five to twelve years old were weighed at the start of the camp and again before they were sent home, to see how much weight they had gained. I loved taking part. We told bedtime stories from the Bible. Some of the children gave their hearts to the Lord. After they returned home, we held reunions once or twice in the Central High School garden grounds with the permission of Rev Bugicanian and Rev Salibian. I kept in touch with them for a number of years.

In the hospital children's ward

I happened to care for a young boy called John Sagherian. He was the son of the hospital chaplain. I used to babysit for this family when Pastor and his wife, Ellen, went to pressing church committee meetings; they used to call me to babysit for their two, then three, children, Pauline, John and Knar. (Calvin arrived later.) I used to tell them bedtime Bible stories. John was a good reader and was reading Jungle Pilot books written by

Dr Paul White, a British missionary to Africa. I must have told his family about my ambition because John, knowing a little about my desire, kept calling me, "Auntie Ovsanna, you must read these books by Dr Paul White."

I was very busy with my studies and told John, "Not now, one day I will."

"No," he would insist and begged me to read. So I did take a book and read it; I loved it and decided to write to Dr Paul White and ask him what I had to do to become a missionary. Dr Paul replied, advising me to take up midwifery, and said, "If it's the Lord's will, He will melt the difficulties like a candle."

My career was taking direction – to become a Bible woman, a midwife and then a missionary. I was not going to marry, full stop.

Reverend Lazarian comes from America to help in the Bible Seminar

Reverend Lazarian, a retired minister, had come voluntarily to help in the newly-formed Bible Seminary in Bethel, a parcel of land purchased by Rev S Doctorian.

Rev Lazarian became my patient. This was his second admission for a hernia operation. Because he was a key member of the Bible school, each time I took his meals I used to ask him questions about how I could become a candidate. He used to encourage me and before I left his room I often asked him to lay his hand on me and pray for me. He reassured me that my name would be in their book as soon as I graduated from the Christian Medical Centre (CMC) Hospital.

Rev Lazarian had known of a lady many years ago whose name was Mariam Varjabedian. He asked whether I knew such a person in the Armenian community. I was surprised to hear from him my grandmother's name. I said, "Mariam Bajie Varjabedian happens to be my grandmother." I asked him how he knew her.

He told me that Mariam Bajie (Bajie means sister) had a donkey and used to distribute eye treatment solution. The young Mr Lazarian was newly married when he and his wife arrived in Beirut with some other refugees. They needed help getting their belongings carried to the Beirut seaport so that they could emigrate to America. It was this widowed lady, Mariam Varjabedian, who helped to carry his wife and their parcels of belongings on the donkey's back to the seaport. He desired to meet her and thank her for the kindness they had received so long ago. I arranged this meeting. He was so excited, he wrote and brought his wife from America to meet my grandmother. Not only this, Mrs Lazarian wished to adopt me and take me to America. She was thinking and planning this venture, but it was not to be. God had other plans for my life.

Wrist tattoo is a sign of pilgrimage to the Holy City of Jerusalem

My eldest brother Jacob got engaged to a lovely lady called Anjel. In the Middle East it is a long-standing custom for couples to have blood tests before getting engaged. Both the man and the woman had to provide blood test results to the church authority as proof that they were free of venereal diseases.

So Miss Anjel came to the hospital clinic to give a blood sample for analysis. I was in the clinic with the doctor who took the blood sample. As I was rolling up her sleeve to apply the tourniquet I noticed Anjel had a small tattoo on her forearm. I asked her when had she been to Jerusalem. She said, "When I was a baby in arms, my dad and mum were travelling through Jerusalem; they had been tattooed themselves, they thought they would tattoo me too." You never know when you might have another chance to pass through Jerusalem.

As she was telling me her story, I was praying, speaking to the Lord about the desire of my heart (Psalm 37:4). It was a silent prayer felt from the very depth of my heart. I must mention that my desire was not to have a tattoo, no, but to see Calvary where Jesus had paid my debt and the empty tomb.

Not long after this incident, a gentleman short in stature came to the hospital and announced to the nurses that there was going to be a tour of Jerusalem. A charter aeroplane had been arranged for a five-day pilgrimage. Those who wished to join were invited to give their names, fill in the form and hand it to him. He would arrange legal documents for the passports and permission for entry to Jerusalem. Mr Joseph, a male nurse, and I were the only ones who applied to join this pilgrimage.

The tour was for five days. I was on night duty at the time. (We worked 28 days, nine hours each night, without a day off in between; we had four days off at the end of each month.) I asked one of my friends to work one extra day for me, and I would work one extra day for her. This was agreed.

All those who were going gathered together at the Brethren Church. We were taken to Beirut airport and an hour-and-a-half later we touched down in Jerusalem. At the airport there was a strange-looking lady guard, dressed in army uniform. Rev Samuel Doctorian said she was an Armenian who had worked in the airport for years, but would not let others know she was a Christian.

The hotel where we stayed was called David's Hotel, near Via Dolorosa, the cobbled narrow streets where Jesus had carried the heavy cross to his death. One of the ladies in the group was so excited when she saw a donkey tied up nearby, she asked, "Is this the donkey on which Jesus rode?" I think it is a must for any Christian to visit Jerusalem. The Bible becomes alive when you see the places Jesus walked and taught.

Rev Samuel was our guide. He had lived in Jerusalem when he was a young boy. It was here in Jerusalem that he had received his call to evangelise the world! He took us to all the most historic places and read from the Bible appropriate chapters. He took us to where the sycamore tree had been on which Zacchaeus had climbed to see Jesus passing by. It was very funny to see the shortest gentleman amongst us (who organised our passports) climbing up the sycamore tree and Rev Samuel acting as Jesus: "Zacchaeus come down from the tree, for I am coming to your house for tea." When Zacchaeus jumped down from the tree, we clapped and took some pictures.

We were taken to the Garden of Gethsemane, the Dome

of the Rock, Calvary Hill and the tomb of Joseph of Arimathaea. In the Calvary garden we had prayers and sang hymns. I shall never forget as we entered the empty tomb in small groups. It felt as if the place we were standing in was shaking. There we felt the resurrection power of God.

Rev Samuel fell face down and prayed aloud with tears. He asked for a broadcasting studio from where he could broadcast in several languages the good news to all those in the Middle East. A few years later, all he had asked for came to pass. "Delight yourself in the LORD and He will give you the desires of your heart" (Psalm 37:4).

Baptism in the River Jordan

On Friday there were seven candidates for water baptism in the River Jordan. We had to have early breakfast, get ready to go to the Jordan River area and have a picnic under booths. After breakfast, everyone went to his or her room to get ready. I stayed at my place. A group of elders were in the corner of the restaurant, planning the day's activity. I was left alone, praying quietly, "Lord, I would love to be baptised." The church I attend does not baptise in water; water is sprinkled on the foreheads of those who are to be baptised, but I had seen some other churches where they baptised in water, and I had always wondered why our church did not. It is written in the Scriptures, "Whoever believes and is baptised will be saved" (Mark 16:16).

I was talking to the Lord from inside my heart, "I am the youngest in the group and am very shy to ask or do anything about it, let someone ask me if you think I am ready to be baptised." Behold, these words were still in my thoughts when one of the elders came from behind me, put his hand on my shoulder and asked, "Would you like to be baptised?" I was so overwhelmed by the prompt answer to my deep longing, I said, "Oh, yes please."

> *"Before they call I will answer; while they are still speaking I will hear."*
>
> *(Isaiah 65:24)*

I ran down the corridor to my friends' room. They were ready to go. I told them what had happened – I was accepted for the baptism. Alice said, "I feel ill. I don't feel well enough to go into the river." She had been baptised a month ago in the church. "Really, it is selfish of me to be baptised so soon again, you can have my gown. Here take it and wear it when you get there." So I took the gown with me.

We arrived at the banks of the River Jordan. They chose the area where allegedly Jesus had been baptised. They tied a thick rope to the trunk of a tree. All those who were to be baptised lined up, each one had to give their testimony, then enter the river by holding the thick rope. Rev Samuel said, "On the confession of your faith, I baptise you in the Name of the Father and of the Son and of the Holy Spirit." Then he immersed them in the fast running muddy waters of the River Jordan.

I stood watching them going down one at a time after giving their testimony. I was concerned about how I was going to clean myself after coming out of the muddy waters of the River Jordan. I only had one small towel to dry myself with, the others were better prepared and had larger towels.

At last my turn had come. I noticed Rev Lazarian, who had sat with me in the aeroplane, going into the water to baptise me, together with Rev Samuel. They were both ready to receive me after my testimony. I told them I was from an underprivileged family. I cried out to God, "I need your help." As I called, I remembered the day I had invited Jesus into my heart by preparing a seat for Jesus to come and reign there.

As I was telling my testimony, God was revealing his wisdom to me. Had I been a child from a rich family, I would not have found the Lord. I began to understand that God in His wisdom had placed me where it was best for me. "Seek first His kingdom and His righteousness, and all these things will be given to you" (Matthew 6:33).

I held the rope and took one step into the river. It felt like stepping into soft yoghurt up to my waist. The second step I took, I felt the strong current of fast running water. I was in the middle of the narrow river by this time. Rev Lazarian repeated the words, "On the confession of your faith I baptise you in the Name of the Father, and of the Son and of the Holy Spirit." They held me firmly, immersed me and got me up. I walked back holding the rope, stood by the river bank looking for mud to clean from my foot. There was no sign of mud, I stood amazed. I heard the Holy Spirit say, "What are you looking for? Your sins which were many, like mud, are washed away, you are clean." I felt in my soul a tremendous peace.

I was using a white towel to dry myself and afterwards I could not see any spots of mud on it. This revelation has lived with me ever since. Mr Joseph took some pictures of us. He later told me that I had looked like an angel as I stood pondering! It was a compliment.

> *"Peter replied, 'Repent and be baptised, every one of you, in the name of Jesus Christ for the forgiveness of your sins. And you will receive the gift of the Holy Spirit.'"*
>
> (Acts 2:38)

Looking forward to my graduation

Humbled yet strengthened, I returned from my extraordinary pilgrimage to Jerusalem to the ups and downs of hospital life. As it was my last year, the year of exams, I was looking forward to the graduation so that I could join the Bible school at Peniel Seminary. Rev Lazarian had promised to have my name on the waiting list.

I was so curious to learn more about how the organs in the human body work and interact, how they got damaged, how they could be treated; in short, I enjoyed every aspect of my career as a nurse. This was partly due to my being in charge of the clinic at nights, when the doctors were away. Whenever a patient arrived at the hospital gate I had to roughly assess the main reason for the patient's complaint, then telephone the doctor on duty and give him a possible diagnosis. This would give me the incentive to check if I had been right in the description I had given to the GP.

At the final exam, we had to go through oral, practical

and written exams. The four of us – Nevart, Jane, Shooshig and I – did well and passed. The graduation was the highlight of three years of hard work and study. It was held in the hospital grounds, in the garden. A platform was set up, the Lebanese flag was displayed, seats were lined up and cards reserving seats for distinguished personnel were put in place. The audience arrived. Everyone stood while the national anthem was played and loudspeakers echoed every imaginable sound. We received our hard-earned Nursing Diplomas. From now on we were State Registered Nurses. That was it – the excitement was over. Three of my colleagues left for work in another hospital.

I waited two months for my career to start. No sign of a letter from the hospital administrator, to say whether I was staying or not. So I picked up my courage and knocked at the door of his office. I was asked in, and presented him with my question. "Where is my letter of leave? I thought you had forgotten."

"No," he retorted, "You were given a form to sign at the start of your training, asking you to stay a further twelve months. You would be paid a salary of 100 Lebanese pounds. We have your signature here." He pulled out a file and showed me my signature. I was most surprised that I had forgotten that occasion.

Later, when I thought back, I remembered the occasion. It was our first anatomy test quiz; we were all anxious, not knowing what to expect. Doctor Ishkhanian walked in, handed slips of paper to each one of us and said, "Mr Badeer asks you to sign this, all of you." We all signed, thinking it had to do with our first lesson. Then he collected the slips of paper, without giving us a chance to read, nor did he give any explanation. None of us knew what we were signing.

All this meant that I was not going to be allowed to join the Bible school that I was so hoping to start in September. It was a newly-opened Seminary in our town, so I wouldn't need to go to another country to study theology and become a Bible woman. I had thought this facility had been God's open door for me.

In a couple of days, I went back to Mr Badeer's office and

expressed my wish to leave the hospital. I believed I should join the Bible school. The administrator was straight and hard. I quoted Bible verses, and said, "I want to serve the Lord and listen to Him." When Mr Badeer gave me other quotations from the Scriptures, I would say, "It's better to serve God rather than man." He would defend his action with another verse. I felt utterly humiliated that I could not gain his permission to leave the hospital. He said, "We did not train you for the Bible school, we trained you as a nurse." I gave in; it was no good arguing.

I went down to my room and packed my suitcase, ready to go and speak to someone who would understand my feelings better than Mr Badeer could.

I had an elderly friend within the hospital called Hayganoosh Bajie. She had no one to live with, so she lived with Doctor Krikorian's family, because the doctor had saved her life from breast cancer. She devoted her life to looking after the doctor's family. She became one of them, cooked for them and helped with general household tasks – she became like a granny to them. I was occasionally asked to mind the children, when the work became too heavy for Hayganoosh to cope with.

Therefore Hayganoosh and I had a good relationship. She had become my spiritual mother and prayer partner, and nearly every day, when I used to go to the Chapel to practise my piano lesson, Hayganoosh would join me there for prayer. We valued those moments of quiet prayer together. Before I took any steps out of the hospital I therefore shared my stressful situation with Hayganoosh Bajie. I listened to her, and we prayed. Soon she let Mr Badeer know about my intention. The news got to Auntie Vergine Badeer.

I wanted to see Mr Samuel Pashigian, a professional sign writer, an experienced, long-standing Sunday school superintendent and also the father-in-law of Rev Samuel Doctorian, who was the director of the newly opened Bible school Seminary. Mr Pashigian was also on the advisory committee of this seminary.

On Monday at about one o'clock in the afternoon I left the

hospital to consult Mr Pashigian, in the hope that he might act as a mediator between me and Mr Badeer, and somehow make it possible for me to obtain leave from the hospital, so that I might start Bible school in September.

> *"Do not be wise in your own eyes; fear the LORD and shun evil."*
>
> Proverbs 3:7

As soon as I was outside, on the steps by the hospital gate, I met Auntie Vergine Badeer (she was the wife of the administrator). We greeted one another. Mrs Badeer was going in the same direction as I was, so we walked together right up to Doctor Badeer's house. Mrs Vergine was going to visit her mother-in-law, Mrs Persape Badeer, and I was going a little further down the side street to meet with Mr Samuel Pashigian. As we walked Aunt Vergine tried to assure me that they needed me at the hospital because of staff shortages, saying that I could think about joining Bible school the following year. (I had the feeling that aunt Vergine was praying for my rebellious spirit to change.) We said goodbye and she went up to see her mother-in-law, while I turned the corner into the side street, where Mr Samuel Pashigian lived.

With prayerful heart and some trepidation, I rang the doorbell. Mr Pashigian opened the door and asked me in. I told him why I was distressed, that I had had high hopes of starting Bible school that September, but that Mr Badeer would not let me because I had signed a contract form three years earlier, of which I had no recollection.

Mr Samuel welcomed me in, and was pleased to have been at home to help advise me. Normally he would have been at work, but that day it was exceptional for him to have been at home. For two hours he tried to give me lots of examples from his own experience of working life. He told me how he had had to submit to his various masters in his sign-writing career.

One of his bosses had been an unbeliever who paid very poor wages. Some of Samuel's friends who were also sign-writers had asked him to join them for much higher wages, saying, "You need the money to feed your five growing children and provide them with schooling." Some had even offered four times as much to get him to work for them. But Samuel would not change his mind, he had remained faithful to the one boss for many long years.

Samuel's friends had ridiculed him, but it had not affected his determination to stay on and be faithful to his employer. He had shown him the love of Christ and, by remaining faithful, he had kept his integrity. Later his boss had moved to Turkey, leaving Samuel in charge of the business; and when Mr Pashigian's master eventually died, Samuel had inherited the whole business.

The two hours soon passed; I learned quite a lot listening to all that he had to say. One most important lesson I learned was to stay faithful wherever God had placed me at the time. He also said that even if I became the most successful and loved Bible woman and had only hurt one person, that person was enough to spoil my reputation. In short, "Go and submit to your higher authorities."

I came out of his presence as a lamb, wanting not my will but God's will to be done. This was an act of dying to self. As Paul the Apostle said, "Consider yourselves as dead, and alive to Christ."

> *"For you died, and your life is now hidden with Christ in God."*
>
> (Colossians 3:3)

I left Mr Samuel Pashigian's home with a sense of 'being in the Master's presence'.

> *"'Go down to the potter's house, and there I will give you my message.' So I went down to the potter's house, and saw him working at the wheel. But the pot he was shaping from the clay was marred in his hands; so the potter formed it into another pot, shaping it as seemed best to him."*
>
> (Jeremiah 18:2-4)

So I am in God's hand, I thought to myself.

I made my way straight to the Christian Medical Centre Hospital, unpacked my suitcase, put on my uniform and cap, went up to the ward, did all that there was to be done, putting behind me all that rebellious spirit, submitting to the authorities, putting self to death!

> *"We have all had human fathers who disciplined us and we respected them for it. How much more should we submit to the Father of our spirits and live! Our fathers disciplined us for a little while as they thought best; but God disciplines us for our good, that we may share in His holiness. No discipline seems pleasant at the time, but painful. Later on, however, it produces a harvest of righteousness and peace for those who have been trained by it."*
>
> Hebrews 12:9-11

We had to have a new uniform and badge once we had graduated. Now I was a qualified State Registered Nurse earning a salary of 100 Lebanese pounds a month. I had to work one month on night duty in charge, four days off duty, then the following month on day duty. I was given a single room, which I appreciated as it enabled me to sleep without disturbance during the day.

The political situation in Beirut was beginning to get serious. We did not know much about what was happening outside the hospital, but there were sporadic gunshots heard as soon as the sun went down. It was 1959.

We used to get the injured. I remember one occasion, a man was carried in who had been shot in the chest and abdomen. An emergency operation got under way. Then his brother came through the hospital gates, straight to see his brother, but his brother was in the theatre being operated on. Doctors were trying to save his brother's life. This man was so furious he began to kick the theatre door. I was trying to restrain him. Here God intervened. The man fainted and fell onto the floor outside the theatre door. I do not know what would have happened if he had carried on kicking. You see

God is in control of our lives, if we could only see His mighty acts and give Him the praise due to Him.

The injured man died through his injuries, due to heavy loss of blood, but the relatives were so angry, threatening the doctor's life. So the doctor wrote a statement and went into hiding that same night. The staff in the CMC hospital had a very tough time for nearly 17 years during the Lebanese civil war. I think God took me out of that war situation, by leading me to England.

Coach accident

The following year the Armenian Evangelical Church School had a sad loss of young lives through a coach accident. The Central High School principal had organised a football competition with Ainjar village Armenian Evangelical High School. This trip was an annual activity for the schools. Central High School took four coaches full of pupils to Ainjar for this match. They won the game, and were returning from this village school in the Bekaa Valley. As they crossed through the high Lebanon Mountains, one of the new coaches must have had a faulty clutch, so the teacher suggested that they get out of the coach so that the clutch could be checked. After a thorough check they were given the all clear.

They got back into the coach with a peaceful mind. But as the coach was coming down a steep mountain road, it went out of control and hit the balcony of a house. The roof of the bus was sliced off, so those who were in the way were killed, 24 young boys and girls, amongst them two small children, and one teacher (the deputy principal).

I was in the hospital chapel, practising my piano lesson. Sister Zulauf came running to inform me of the sad news. The Central High School graduate class had all perished! It was world news. We waited for the injured to be brought to the hospital, but there were none. Two boys aged 16 had sustained minor injuries and had asked passing cars to give them a lift to CMC Hospital. There were two others with serious injuries.

Later that evening, there was such pandemonium at the school gates; the parents were so outraged with the principal, he had to look after his own safety. The pastor's eldest son was among the dead. His sister, Araxie, asked me to go to their home and stay the night with her. I kept company with Araxie because we were friends, as well as being related.

My brother-in-law visited all the churches in the region, suggesting this had been a trumpet call from God to hold revival meetings, caring and sharing with the bereaved families, but there was no response. The church members split and it was the most sad and painful time for the whole of the community. There were two severely injured pupils who suffered spinal injuries, one of whom transferred to Stoke Mandevlle Hospital in England. Even in these sorts of times, God is working his purposes for the good of mankind. We will not know until we meet with Him.

Encounter with Miss Betts

Very occasionally the weather in Beirut gets cold: it snows and the traffic stops. One such day Miss Betts, a nursing sister, had come to Beirut for a council administration meeting being held in the town centre hall. It was late in finishing. Doctor Krikorian brought her with him, to stay the night in CMC. I was asked if I could give my room to Miss Betts (who was the matron of the Sanatorium Hospital). I gladly did so, and went and slept with the student nurses downstairs in the nurses' dormitory.

In the morning, at the breakfast table, Miss Betts talked about her need for nurses to work in the Sanatorium. It is hard to find nurses who are willing to work in a TB hospital because there is a stigma attached to it. Because it is a contagious disease not many parents allow their daughters to take up employment in a sanatorium. I knew of two nurses who were looking for a job. Miss Betts was interested to meet with those nurses, so we made an appointment to go and visit them.

Miss Betts was successful in recruiting them for the jobs. This is how I became friendly with her. (She was an Irish nurse trained in London). In the course of our conversation Miss Betts asked me what my future plans were. Very tentatively I replied, "I would love to study further, obtain midwifery training, and become a missionary."

She knew quite a few hospitals in London and said she would be glad to find a good training school for me in England. She left me with this hope before she went back to the Azuniah Sanatorium.

I knew the Azunia Sanatorium well. I had spent three months of my third year training there to gain experience in chest surgery. I had thoroughly enjoyed my time there, had made good friends and enjoyed the snow-capped mountain air. I had taken groups of patients on picnics and had also eaten healthy meals.

Towards the end of the second year I was working as a staff nurse in charge of night and day duty, alternate months. I became anxious that I had not heard from Miss Betts regarding her promise of finding a nursing training school in London. I had waited three long months and I gave up expecting anything of her promise.

One day I went to my room to sleep, as I had been on night duty that night. From a quite unexpected source, one of the laundry ladies said, "Did you hear the news?"

"What?" I asked.

"The Bible school that you wished to enter has been closed down by the Government." Well, that was indeed news to me.

Then I realised that the two years of staff nursing in the CMC had not been wasted.

One bright Sunday afternoon. The hospital chaplain, Rev Sagherian, came to visit the patients. He was trying to find a few moments to talk with me. He stopped me and said, "I have a letter to answer, to a lady called Arpine Domburian. She has been waiting for a reply from me for six months. She asked me if I could give her a reference letter, to enable her to start nursing in one of the London hospitals. He continued. "Would you like me to write a few lines about you?"

I was so pleased to hear what Rev Sagherian said. I said, "Thanks! Yes, do so please."

A few days later, Rev Sagherian received a letter. When he opened the envelope, he found some application forms from the King Edward Memorial (KEM) Hospital in Ealing, West

London. He knew it was a response to his letter to Miss Arpine Dombourian.

Miss Dombourian had by now started nursing in Ealing KEM Hospital. So it was quite a miracle how I received the application forms. Her kindness in showing the letter about me from Rev Sagherian to the matron of the KEM Hospital had resulted in my receiving them. The forms were passed on to me and after a careful thought and prayer, I filled them in, giving all the details required, and posted the application.

I had two weeks of annual leave. As usual I went to Kchag Summer Camp to help with the 150 undernourished children from around the towns. While I was there I received a letter from the King Edward Memorial Hospital informing me that my application had been accepted, and that the forthcoming studies would be starting on 29th September 1960. As you can imagine I was over the moon, telling everyone that I would be going in few weeks.

Rev Lazarian once again came to CMC Hospital in Beirut. He asked me if I had heard about the Bible school closing down. I told him that I had, through casual conversation with a laundry lady. I shared with him how the Lord was opening another avenue of service for me in England. He was pleased and he prayed for God's blessing and guidance over me.

In the Brethren Church, there was a young intelligent man who had become a concert conductor at an early age. He held a musical concert, depicting 'the last seven words of Jesus while on the cross'. I was present at one of these concerts. His name was Michael. After his high school graduation he had secured a job at the Beirut airport.

Michael came to visit Rev Lazarian. Immediately I thought of asking him if he could guide me in buying an air ticket to get to England. Before he left I stopped and put my request to him. He told me, "There are so many airlines, do you know which one you prefer?"

I told him, "I do not know anything about flights."

He said, "I will bring you a list, and you have to choose. I'll be coming on Friday to visit Rev Lazarian." We met on Friday and chose the Lebanese airline.

I continued working at nights. As I have mentioned, after 28 days of night work we used to get four days off, so I used one of the four days off to visit Azunieh Sanatorium Hospital, to go and see Miss Betts and tell her all that the Lord was doing regarding further training in England.

Miss Betts was so pleased, she asked me if I was free to meet her on Monday at 12.30pm in Beirut town centre in front of the De Luxe restaurant. I agreed to keep the appointment. We met, she took me into the restaurant and we had the most delicious ice cream. Then she took me to a large warehouse, full of all sorts of suitcases. She chose a large but lightweight suitcase with secure locks, and paid 40 Lebanese pounds. She showed me this kindness, I presume, because in the course of my conversation I had told her about my mother buying me a suitcase which weighed seven kilograms, too heavy for travelling with. This suitcase story has a very significant place to play in my testimony. It became my companion for many years. Miss Betts gave me some very useful advice about English currency and where to do my shopping; she encouraged me to buy clothing from charity shops etc.

The second day off I took a public transport bus to the village where my sister's family and my brother's family were both spending the summer. To escape the scorching heat of the town they had come to the higher altitudes of Beitmery village, where the air was much cooler. I stayed the night at my sister's rented flat, in the same village as the rest of the relatives. During the day I visited my younger brother, Bedros (Peter). Bedros and Anahid had their first baby boy, lovely Hrach, who was six months old. I played with the baby, and spent a happy and relaxed time with my sister-in-law, sharing with her all the blessings that I was receiving.

Anahid was a very thrifty, intelligent, beautiful and humorous lady. She was a homemaker and very careful with her money. She made my brother sell his car to save on petrol, so that they could buy useful household gadgets. However, I said goodbye at the end of a happy day and returned to my sister's for the night.

On the way home, high up on the mountain top, there

was a large rock. I sat on it and opened my heart to God in prayer, "Lord, there are many issues; from now on my life relies on your provision, guidance and protection. I do not know what the future holds for me but you do know. If it is your will that I should go to England, please provide. When I get to London I will ring the matron and ask her to send me a taxi so that I will not get lost. I will work during my holidays and pay the money I owe to the driver. Amen."

It was a clear sky, the city lights were glittering, and the air was getting chilly, so I hurried back to my sister's home for shelter.

On the fourth day of my days off I got up early, had a quick breakfast, said my goodbyes, and went out to the bus stop where everyone who worked in town had to catch the early morning bus to get to their jobs in time.

Michael (the orchestra conductor), who was now employed by the Lebanese airline, had asked me to meet with his boss at 9am at his office in downtown Beirut. The bus I boarded got me to town in good time. I found the office but it was not yet open, so I waited a few minutes. Michael arrived, opened the office door, took me in, introduced me to his boss and left. (I have difficulty remembering the names of people, but do not forget what they do or say – please forgive me.)

This gentleman sat at his office desk. He was an Arab man so we spoke in Arabic. As soon as I entered the office he put his hand under his desk and pulled out an air ticket. He handed it to me saying, "Here is your ticket to London Heathrow Airport."

I was speechless. I said with trembling voice, "But sir, I have no money with me. I only have 20 piasters (pence) for my bus fare to work."

My legs were like jelly. I was trembling with the shock of having unexpectedly to pay 600 Lebanese pounds for the ticket he was handing me. On hearing this, he replied, "You are a nurse from CMC Hospital. We trust the nurses from the CMC. Pay it before you board the airplane." I took a few steps forward, accepted the ticket and thanked him. I came out of his office burdened with a feeling of huge debt. How was I going to find this amount of money in three to four weeks? (It was six months wages.)

On my way back in the bus I spoke with my heavenly Father in prayer. He is faithful to His word to perform it: "I will do whatever you ask in my name, so that the Son may bring glory to the Father. You may ask me for anything in my name, and I will do it" (John 14:13). I returned to the bus stop, caught the bus back and paid the bus fare with the last 20 piasters left in my pocket. When I arrived at Bourje-Hamoud district I had a good look at the air ticket. To my surprise my own name, my father's name, address and date of birth, were all registered. No one had asked me if they could do this. I did wonder how they had obtained all this information. Later, when I enquired, I was told that Michael's mother knew my mother, so Michael had sent his mother to my mother's house to get all the information.

I went to my older brother's shop (he is a shoemaker).

I showed the ticket to my brother Hagop. He took it from my hand, had a look at it and threw it amongst the dusty piles of shoe moulds. I pleaded with him saying, "Please, if we can't pay, I will take it back." I picked the ticket up, brushed off the dust and went to CMC Hospital to resume work. I had been away for four days and was on evening shift that weekend.

In the days to come, I had to go over my plans with my dad. I told him my intention of leaving for England to study nursing further. I knew he would not agree, nor give me permission to leave the country, so I went back to my brother, who was the breadwinner, to get his consent. Neither he nor Dad would agree.

So I had to bring this situation to God's wisdom and guidance in quiet prayer.

The hospital chaplain, Rev Sagherian, was well loved and respected by my dad and my brother. I approached Rev Sagherian and explained the situation to him and I asked if he would kindly write a note to them, asking them to release me to go to England for my future good. This he did.

I took the letter to my brother because it was addressed to him. He read and calmly said, "Alright, if that's what Rev

Sagherian says. But don't ask me for any money."

I was pleased to hear my brother say that it was all right for me to go, because in the past he had said, "If CMC does not employ you, you sit at home. We do not want a woman to leave home and go to another country." (This is another Middle Eastern custom). Two prayers were answered.

I wrote my notice to leave CMC Hospital. The news of having been given a ticket without having to pay was circulating amongst the staff, but no one at home knew about this, except my brother Hagop (Jacob). I had perfect peace, I trusted and had confidence in God's word. I had asked God for 600 Lebanese pounds so that I could pay before getting on the airplane.

"And my God will meet all your needs according to His glorious riches in Christ Jesus" (Philippians 4:19). With this confidence, and resting on His unfailing love, I went back to the village where my loved ones were living during the summer months, and told them that the ticket was already in my possession without my having to pay. I also told them how I was feeling under a debt. They all knew I had no money in the bank or anywhere else. I also knew: if the Lord is in it, He will do exceedingly better than we think or ask.

Within two weeks, I had double the amount I had asked of God. This is how God supplied it. Each time it was someone's birthday, I loved to give them a gift. But my sister, out of her wisdom, suggested that I give the money to her, so that she could buy what was best for that person. She knew I might spend it if it was left with me. Naomi gave me 250 Lebanese Lira (pounds).

Bedros' wife Anahid gave me 300 Lebanese Lira. One day I visited Anahid in the Bedmery village and played with her six-month-old baby son, Hrach. Then I said goodbye and made my way home. As I was leaving, she came out with me to see me off, gave me a brown envelope and said, "This is the best we could do, please take it and use it, it is only a little help towards your needs, count it as such."

I was really touched by her sweet kindness and thanked her very much. I was not expecting anything from them, because she needed money for the baby's powdered milk. When I got home I opened the envelope and found the 300 Lebanese Lira.

Next I visited Hagop and, when he asked me how I was, I told him that Bedros' wife Anahid had given me 300 Lebanese Lira towards the ticket. Hagop eventually gave me 300 LL, the same as Bedros.

I had not collected my salary from the hospital for two months and that amounted to 200 Lebanese Lira. Grandmother Sultan and Sister Alice Albarian together gave another 250 Lebanese Lira. My Mother gave 100 Lebanese Lira. All this made a total of 1,200 Lebanese Lira, double the amount I had asked of God. The hospital also gave me 50 Lebanese Lira and a wristwatch.

I did not waste any time. I paid the money for the ticket and went to the bank to change the rest of the money into Sterling. This amounted to £79. I knew without a doubt that God was in this journey.

As I got ready to leave I went about seeing friends and relatives. Anahid's dad challenged me, saying, "Once you are in England you may meet with a man and that might be the end of your missionary work." My reply to him was, "I do not think that will happen to me. I am determined to study and become a midwife." Another kindness I must not forget to mention is that Haroutoon, my brother-in-law, made me a nice warm coat and a suit to take with me.

On 27th September 1960 all my dear ones rallied round me in the airport to wish me well and a safe journey. We took a few pictures. I was very conscious about leaving behind my mother and father. They had no income at all, apart from Hagop's generosity. Now Hagop was married and had a son, Raffy. He had moved into new accommodation with his wife Anjel, leaving behind Mum and Dad.

The time came to board the aircraft. I was the last passenger to get board. I found my seat, the next but one nearest to the window. There was a Persian gentleman nearest to the window. I asked him if I could look out of the window before the plane took off. To my great surprise, I spotted my dad in the distance. He was wiping his eyes with a white handker-chief. My heart seared with sorrow. Just as I was sorrowing about leaving my parents behind, I heard the Holy Spirit whisper, "Whether you are in Beirut or in England, you are not the one who cares for your mum and dad; you can leave their care to me." It was so clear, the comforting thought of the Holy Spirit ringing in my soul. "The Spirit Himself testifies with our spirit (within us)" (Romans 8:16).

I released them to the Lord's mighty care. This peace of mind was the best gift and I could not have received it from anyone else. Hearing God speak to us through His Spirit is natural; if the Spirit of God lives in me, it includes walking by faith, trusting God's Word, hearing His voice and obeying the leading of His Spirit (Romans 8:9).

When my sister left home to work in Qatar Hospital in Kuwait, it had broken my heart. Since then, I had had a taste of separation, and each time I saw someone leave I used to cry, as though I had been deserted. This time it was much more painful to leave my dear ones behind while facing the unknown, but God's Spirit was the one I was following. I had put my hand on the plough – no turning back.

I had put my confidence in the Lord, the good shepherd, He was leading me on. "I am the good shepherd; I know my sheep and my sheep know me" (John 10:14).

How did I know He was leading me?

I had not applied to any hospital or chosen the area. The application forms had come into my hands; I had filled them in, sent them and had been accepted.

The ticket had been handed to me without my first paying.

I had had no money to pay for the ticket. 600 Lebanese Lira represented my wages for six months. I had been supplied double what I had asked for in my prayers – 1,200 Lebanese Lira.

A large lightweight suitcase had been given to me to use for my flight.

My concern for the care of my dad and mum had been taken care of by the Holy Spirit. I heard the still small voice say, "Whether you are here or there, you are not the one who takes care of your parents. It is I who take care of them, trust me. The Holy Spirit can be trusted." In spite of my sister's constant opposition to the idea, I was leaving for England.

It was a fine clear humid day on 27th September. The aeroplane left Beirut airport in the afternoon. I can't remember the exact time. We were to land in Rome for refuelling and for passengers to leave and others to join, but the touchdown was extended hour by hour due to a technical fault. We were all getting tired and hungry, and some people were even getting angry. In the end, five hours of delay was proving too long, so we were provided with Italian spaghetti bolognaise. With full stomachs we set off, and after a few hours the pilot announced our descent into London Heathrow Airport.

I was curious to have a look out of the window. It was very dark, as dawn had not yet broken. From the air the city of London looked like a vast area of orderly geometrical lines of orange streetlights, like a glittering blanket covering the sleeping giant of a city!

Touchdown took place at about 4am. After all the passport and suitcase checks we were hurried into a waiting airport bus, each one to be taken to their destination. The airport transport officer introduced me to the home sister at King Edward Memorial Hospital at 6am on the 28th September 1960. So I didn't have to worry about the taxi fare after all!

6
Cultural shock

The driver left from Heathrow Airport at about 5am, when it was still dark. He stopped at every red traffic light; this was a new experience for me as in Beirut there was no traffic light system operating as yet. We were all tired from the overnight journey; we wanted to get to our destination as quickly as possible. I did wonder why the driver was stopping at every red traffic light when there was no one in the road or at the pedestrian crossing. That gave me the impression that there was law and order in England, not like Lebanon, where accidents were a regular occurrence.

The gentleman sitting next to me in the aeroplane was a Persian ophthalmologist (a student of eye disease), and he was also coming to London to study further. We got to know each other during the time we were travelling. I was the last but one to be delivered to my address. The last one was Mr Mohammed.

At the King Edward Memorial Hospital in Ealing the home sister, Miss Wellington, met me and took me to my bedroom to rest and overcome jet lag. The next day, I was taken round the hospital to get to know the departments, get acquainted with the ward set-up, find my way around the hospital, fire escape methods, casualty department, nursing school, lecture room, time tables, rules of the nursing home etc. I also had a medical check-up and filled in and signed various forms. Students were recruited every six months.

The hospital was within walking distance of Ealing Broadway tube station. There were two large parks in the area and a good shopping centre. I went with the new nurses to look round the area and to get to know the shops, availability of hairdressers, churches, cinemas etc. Walpole Park was behind the hospital, and nurses used to go there to relax, play tennis and visit the bird sanctuary and beautiful landscape around the hospital.

Before long we were transferred to another building half-an-hour away, where two nursing school students were to join for six months. Altogether there were 30 students at the West Middlesex Hospital and the King Edward Memorial Hospital. The training department was an hour's walk from the main KEM Hospital. For the first six months we were housed there and given training in basic nursing care. We had three tutors. We received very intensive practical teaching within a classroom setting before we were allowed to work in the wards. This was called preliminary training school (PTS). At the end of it we had to pass oral and written exams.

We had to sign in and sign out each time we wanted to go out. Whenever a few of us went out, it was usually to enjoy ourselves out of sight of strict tutors. We all queued at the fish and chip shop (in those days the best fish and chips were wrapped in newspaper and eaten with fingers). I was quite astonished – I had not thought the English people had such an unhygienic way of eating. When I objected, the sharp answer was, "That's the best way, it tastes much better!"

Another peculiarity I encountered was at mealtimes. All the meals were mashed – mashed potatoes, mashed vegetables, custards and puddings all soft. They had done the chewing for us, as it were! No roughage or fruits, lots of salad cream, tomato sauce and no glasses of cold water. Thankfully, I have never been a fussy eater, so I ate whatever was provided. However, because of the change and anxiety, I became consti-pated for over five days and had to see the sister in charge for a dose of laxative. Once I had taken it, I felt better for it. I enjoyed the course. I knew most of the things, because of my previous study. We all enjoyed the PTS.

At the end of the term, a party was arranged and every-one let their hair down. There was so much excitement, games and modern dancing. They knew how to dance; my word, everyone seemed to know how to dance apart from me. I was totally lost, so I isolated myself, sat further away and enjoyed watching them. It was fun.

We all looked forward to starting work in the hospital. When the day arrived, we were transported to our respective hospitals. There were 17 nurses at KEM hospital and 13 nurses at the West Middlesex.

When we arrived at the Ealing KEM Hospital, each one of us was placed in different departments. I was to work in the women's medical ward for a month, then change to another ward, as planned by the tutor. I got on very well with the senior nurses and the ward sister, and soon got to know the routine running of the wards. I took great pleasure in making friends with the patients too. However, whenever I was off duty, I concentrated on learning anatomy, physiology, signs and symptoms of diseases, treatments, precautions, prevention, drug dosages and how to use medical apparatus.

Whenever I had a day off, I looked for friends to go out with, but they had disappeared with their boy friends or gone home, so I had no one. On Sundays we worked alternate morning and afternoon shifts. Whenever it was my Sunday morning shift, I would try to go to the nearby Baptist church near Ealing Broadway. The Minister was Rev Golden.

The first Sunday I attended was Holy Communion service. I joined them and took part with them. I was overwhelmed with deep joy within my soul. I considered it to be a privilege to partake communion with another nation and language.

"You prepare a table before me in the presence of my enemies. You anoint my head with oil; my cup overflows. Surely goodness and love will follow me all the days of my life, and I will dwell in the house of the LORD for ever."
Psalm 23:5

The church I had left back home used to have Holy Communion only once a year; it was a rare occasion, whereas here in England it was usually once a week.

The Baptist church at Ealing had special cards on the seats

saying, 'If you are a visitor or new to this church, please write your name and address; we will get in touch with you.' I filled in a card each time I went, hoping to meet someone from the church, but unfortunately no one ever got in touch with me during the three years I was living in Ealing.

When I was in the CMC Hospital in Beirut, Lebanon, an elderly retired professor of theology used to visit the patients, and stop and talk to the nurses. I remember him talking with me, challenging me by saying, "99% won't do, you have to be 100% for Christ." He used to write Christian pamphlets on good moral issues from the Bible, print them in large numbers and distribute them to schools, shops and factories. Before I left Beirut, the professor had given me a good number of those pamphlets in English to give away to friends.

On Sundays, whenever I was free and left alone, I had the courage to go out to the end of the street and hand out tracts to passers by. I took pleasure in giving these pamphlets, as it gave me the satisfaction of doing what little I could to serve the Lord I believed in. Sometimes people used to stop and talk; I would take this opportunity to tell them about the Lord Jesus' love of mankind and that He had laid down His life for us all.

I sometimes left literature in the telephone kiosk for people to take home; then I would go and check, to see if it had been taken. Yes, most of the time people did take it with them. I believe some people had nothing much to do on Sunday afternoons. On a cold winter's day, they would use the telephone kiosk to keep warm. Whenever I needed more pamphlets I wrote back home and asked for more to be sent for distribution.

I was a zealous Christian when I first arrived in England. I noticed so much materialism and vanity and pride. I saw Christians doing things that I would not have been allowed to do in my country, but they were getting away with it, so I began to be tempted (for example going to the pictures).

The cold damp weather conditions used to affect my legs; I used to feel as though my bones were freezing. I missed the starry skies; for three months there was no sign of stars in the sky. The cold weather kept me indoors for most of my free time. I was bored, sat at my bedroom window watching the snowfall. There was nothing much to eat in the nurses' tiny kitchen; the shelves were empty, the cornflakes box stood empty and, whenever I found a slice of bread it was not as tasty as the bread we had at home, so I used to eat it sprinkled with salt, because there were no canteens open.

Miss Betts had given me quite a lot of sensible advice, preparing me for the pitfalls when someone is new to a place. She was an experienced lady and I shall never forget what she told me. "You will be like a drop in the ocean!"

All I wanted to do was to pay the sum I owed to the Air Company. As I mentioned before, the ticket cost 600 Lebanese Lira (pounds), which was my salary for six months. I had been given 1200 Lebanese Lira. So, once I had paid the ticket money I owed, I had 600 Lebanese Lira which I changed into travellers' cheques; this made £79 Sterling. So my first step was to open a bank account with the Lloyds Trustee Savings Bank. Mr Perry met me at the counter in the bank, answered all the questions, signed the bank documents, and I handed the £79 to him for safe keeping. Within a few days I received a letter from Mr Perry, the bank clerk. In it he introduced himself and his family to me, and invited me and some Chinese nurses (newcomers into the KEM Hospital) to his home. His invitation was the first kindness we received. It made a great impact on us, as we were feeling 'like drops in the ocean'.

At the weekend we were picked up by Mr Perry and taken to his home, where we met his missionary mother. His parents were veteran missionaries in India and the Middle East. We had a blessed time hearing some of their extraordinary experiences during their mission work. They were such a great blessing to us and to many others.

Each year at Christmas we were invited for meals, parties and the sharing of gifts. They had even made individual Christmas stockings filled with all sorts of useful items. We kept in touch with the Perry family for 40 years.

Sometime later, we were introduced to the Inter Varsity Fellowship. This fellowship used to hold meetings in Central

London for all the foreign students. We were given good advice. For example: "We English are very cold people compared with other nationalities. You have to break the ice and make friends with us. Once you have broken the ice you will find out that we, the British people, are not as cold as you make us out to be."

The Inter Varsity Fellowship also used to arrange for families from churches to keep in touch with a student, so that the student could have a home to turn to in times of crisis or during holidays. I have remained in contact with one such family, the Dallyns, for 46 years. These people do a sterling job.

Life in King Edward Memorial Hospital

Nursing was my vocation; nothing would stop me achieving my purpose which was to do my best, relying on my faith and ambition. Within a few days of my arrival at the KEM Hospital, Miss Arpine Dombourian came along and introduced herself to me. She told me the whole mystery – that she was the lady who had asked Rev Sagherian if he could write a reference letter on her behalf to the Matron of KEM Hospital. (Rev Sagherian was the chaplain of the CMC Hospital in Beirut where I used to work.)

While Arpine was waiting for a reply to her letter from Rev Sagherian she had come to England from Cyprus, to live with her married sister in London. While she was in London she had applied to KEM Hospital for nursing training, had been accepted and had started six months earlier.

When Rev Sagherian had eventually replied to her letter, after a delay of six months, he had mentioned that nurse Ovsanna Bedrossian (that's me) desired to study further nursing. Arpine had had the guts to take the same letter to the matron of the hospital where she was already nursing. On reading the letter, the matron had decided to send me the application forms together with the hospital brochure. This was the mystery I have been talking about. I had not applied, but applications had arrived in my hands, and I had believed this to be an indication of God's guiding plan for me.

The home of the triplets in Ealing

Nurse Arpine and I became good friends. She was six months ahead of me in her training. She had come to know the area and had found out that there was an Armenian couple who had had triplets on the day of my arrival. I was so glad to hear this happy news. We made an arrangement to go and visit them after the mother came out of hospital. The Armenian family lived within walking distance of the hospital. They lived on the second floor. In the same building, on the first floor, lived an Armenian widow, whose name was Manoushag. Auntie Manoushag became our grandmother; we used to go to her whenever we had any problems, she was a good counsellor to us all.

This Armenian family became a focal point of entertainment for the few of us who had come from abroad; it was a home from home. They provided us with a loving home atmosphere – we needed them and they needed us. They had a very large pram which needed quite a few hands to push it. When the mother wanted the babies to be given fresh air and sunshine they called us to give them a helping hand. We used to love taking the babies to the park – it was great fun.

The hospital authorities began to recruit several girls from Lebanon. It seemed they had obtained my address from some mysterious person. All eight of them were unhappy as far as the nursing was concerned; two of them managed to stay, the rest could not continue.

As nurses we were paid £20 a month to cover our basic needs. Most of this money was used to buy minced meat – sixpence bought nearly two pounds of meat. We cooked it with some stuffed aubergines. We only did this once, just to make us feel at home and to overcome our homesickness!

One day one of the girls came to my room crying. "Why did we come to England?" she lamented.

I said, "None of you asked me what life in England was like. If any one of you had written to me before coming, I would have told you the difficulties I was experiencing. Perhaps that would have stopped you coming. I had not come of my own choice, it was the guidance of God's plan. God had provided for all my needs. The ticket was given into my hand and the money followed."

Nurse Ruth's dad was always wishing to come to England to see the Armenian Bible, the oldest manuscript in the British Museum. Before leaving Beirut he wrote and asked his daughter what she would like him to bring with him. She wrote back and asked her dad to bring some Armenian smoked sausages made with a large amount of garlic in them.

The day arrived and we were really looking forward to the appearance of these provisions so that we could all have an oriental feast with the appetising taste and smell of garlic and pepper. You only need one bite of this sausage and it was enough to make your mouth smell horrible.

Ruth went to work after enjoying a few bites. She was on duty in the maternity ward that afternoon. When they were in the office listening to the ward report the ward sister smelt her breath and sent her out of the ward saying, "Go and wash your mouth and run four times around the hospital periphery, then come back."

Ruth came to my room feeling absolutely humiliated, crying her eyes out for being belittled before the other nurses. We often spoke about this incident and laughed about it, and from that time on we were very careful whenever we ate such garlicky stuff. Not only that, we never again asked anyone to bring such food within the hospital annexe. The Chinese nurses also used to bring their special meals, but I don't think they were ostracised as we were.

Children's ward

When it was my turn to work in the children's ward, staff nurse Margaret was in charge of the children's ward. On my first day in the ward staff nurse said, "Miss Bedrossian, you have the same accent as my friend Verkiné Jizmejian. Do you mind if I ask you where you come from?"

I replied, "I come from Beirut in Lebanon, I am of Armenian nationality." She was pleased to hear that I was from Beirut. She then went on to tell me that Verkiné was her best friend and that they had done their nursing training together. She said that Verkiné had a pleasant nature, was humorous, generous and a good cook. When Margaret was getting ready for her wedding Verkiné had made her wedding dress. I asked her where Verkiné was now and she told me that she was in Scotland doing her midwifery training.

I began to communicate with Verkiné and invited her to come and stay with me during her holidays, which she was pleased to do. I gave her my bed to sleep in and I slept on the cushions in the lounge. Whenever I was on duty, I left her to enjoy her hobby of dressmaking, which she was happy to do.

That weekend Verkiné and I were invited for lunch at Margaret's house in Southhall. She and her husband lived in her mother's house, on the first floor. They were saving money to buy their own home eventually. By this time they had been married for three years. Margaret's husband was a Sunday school Superintendent at their Brethren Church. He was running the nurses' Christian Union at KEM Hospital, and was also the secretary and treasurer of the Borneo Faith Mission supported by his church.

On that Sunday Verkiné and I enjoyed a lively meal at Margaret's home. It was wintry cold weather. Her husband had lit the log fire in their lounge. We had roast chicken and as we threw the bones into the fire they sizzled away. In the course of our warm fellowship the conversation turned to her husband going into hospital the following day, Monday morning, to have a minor nasal polyp removed from his nose.

I happened to be working in the men's surgical ward that month. Margaret's husband arrived, was admitted and prepared for theatre. Two porters wheeled him away from the ward and, as they were moving him, there was quite a bit of witty talk going on between them. The other patients overheard it, and it must have been a funny joke as they all laughed aloud.

It was mealtime in the ward. All of a sudden the mood of the ward staff changed. The news of the last patient taken into theatre was very grim. Matron was on the phone calling for help from a leading hospital; a top heart specialist had to come for an emergency resuscitation. The patient's heart had stopped beating, due to the wrong solution being injected into his nose!

This operation was to be carried out while the patient was in a sitting position. He must have been conscious, as his last words were, "I feel sorry for those who undergo a major operation." This is what a Chinese nurse told me; she had been in the theatre at the time when the patient's breathing had stopped. The surgeon was only an ear, nose and throat surgeon, but there was no time to waste. He had to proceed with open cardiac massage with gloved hands while waiting for the heart surgeon to take over (the heart defibrillator was not in use in those days).

Margaret was informed of the catastrophe. On hearing this, I ran to my room to fetch Verkiné to come and be with Margaret. Verkiné's presence in the hospital was timely as no one was closer to Margaret than Verkiné. Matron was out of her mind, she was up and down the hospital concourse, urging the nurses to go into the chapel and pray to God.

I believe that the cause was the relationship between the nurse and the surgeon – they were in love with each other and were both in the middle of divorces from their partners. They had both failed to check the drug being aspirated into the syringe.

The patient was brought into the ward under an oxygen tent. Sadly he only lived 23 hours, then died. Margaret had to give up working. After much legal wrangling, she refused the 'blood ransom' offered to her. During the course of much sorrow and heartache she decided to join Radcliff Bible College.

Nurses' Christian Union

After the funeral, Miss Mary Wang was appointed to become the representative of the Nurses' Christian Union. Mary was a strong believer in a miracle-working God. She was a woman of faith, a persecuted pastor's daughter, trained to become a doctor in north China, but the Chinese authorities would not let her qualify as a doctor because she would not deny God. She was a wonderful pianist, a highly intelligent, God-fearing, precious lady. She knew her Bible well, she could preach and teach, I was privileged to call her my friend in the Lord.

Mary had the spiritual well-being of the student nurses in her heart. We used to gather fortnightly to have fellowship and hear her give inspiring, encouraging messages. She always helped to uplift our spirits. The Chinese nurses considered her as their mentor.

There were so many Chinese students in London that Pastor Steven Wang and Mary came together and formed a youth group. There was a newly formed Chinese church in London. First they used to hold meetings in the YMCA centre but soon they increased in numbers and had their own building.

Pastor Steven Wang had had to leave his country because of persecution. His wife and daughter had been put into prison because of their faith in Jesus Christ. Mary knew the suffering and the heartache Pastor Wang was carrying. Mary used to visit him from time to time, to help him with cleaning, washing, ironing and cooking. (They had the same surname but they were not related.) Mary used to ask me to go with her. I joined her a few times. Pastor Wang often came to take the Nurses' Christian Fellowship and helped to advise the nurses when they needed spiritual counselling.

There came a time when they launched a large Chinese Youth Conference in Hatfield in Middlesex, where Watchman Nee was invited to speak to the young students. I attended and spent a week of my holiday at this conference. It was the highlight of the conference when Watchman Nee spoke. He spoke with such humility. I saw Christ speaking to us through his lips. This was an experience I shall never forget; we all humbled ourselves before the presence of His glory; what a man of God! We came away refreshed, strengthened in the things of God, strong to resist the temptations that this world presents.

The newly formed Chinese church had a good relationship with Rev Doctorian. Whenever Samuel was in London they invited him to preach and showed him great hospitality. The ministers were great friends and they travelled together to Beirut. Pastor Wang desired to meet my parents, to get to know them and pass my love and greetings to them. The reason I am mentioning this is because a couple of years later, when I got engaged, I was concerned as to who I could ask to marry me, and in which church. Because I was living in another country I was not a permanent member of any of the churches where I attended, so I had to choose someone.

I approached Pastor Wang because he had met my parents and had some idea about my background. When I asked him, he was pleased to conduct the whole of the wedding in the borrowed Welsh Church in Baker Street, near Madame Tussauds in London. They would not accept money, so I made a very small gift of a pair of socks to Pastor Wang. The wedding was free.

Sickness and convalescence

Towards the end of six months training I was experiencing pain, especially in the area of my lower back, which was causing concern; also I was underweight. A throat swab revealed that I had a bacterial infection.

The home sister advised me to stay in my room and not to come into contact with any other nurses. Meanwhile I was being given a full course of antibiotics; my temperature was monitored and some tests were carried out to find the cause. This meant that during all this time I was missing class work. My temperature was not coming down, so they admitted me into a nurses' sick bay. When the doctor gave me the all clear they arranged for me to have a period of convalescence for a fortnight in Margate in Kent. It was a seaside nursing home for nurses who fall ill. I was very well cared for and I enjoyed my stay at the seaside.

On my return from Margate Convalescent Home, sister tutor met me with an exam application form to be filled in and sent off. I was the last student who had to fill in the form and sign it in order to sit the Part One Exam. Sister tutor read the form to me. When she came to the last line where it said, 'any student who sits this exam must not be absent more than three days during the course of six months,' she refused to sign it as I had been sick over two weeks. This was a great disappointment to me; it meant I had to lose six months.

The following day I went to see the matron and brought my case to her. I explained to her that though I may have been ill more than three days there should be a compromise in my case, because I had had repeated nursing training. Matron agreed with me and said, "We have been getting good reports from the ward sisters about your work in the wards." (Well I never!) The sister tutor misunderstood this action of mine. The matron called the sister tutor and explained to her that they could allow me to sit this Part One Exam and that I did not need to lose another six months because I had missed classes.

The next day, sister tutor came down the corridor of the lecture hall. I could tell she was full of fury towards me as she said, "You have gone and complained about me to the matron." This was not true – I don't know what happened between the two of them. Obviously Matron must have blamed the tutor for not considering my circumstances and made her sign my application for the exam. This was a very hot potato for her to swallow! From that day onwards tutor made my life very difficult. I dare not tell you how! Nevertheless I sat my exam and passed. I continued praying for two-and-a-half years for God to mend our relationship in the classroom.

Here is just one example. My friend Dietrich, a Swedish nurse, came to me and asked if I could explain to her foetal circulation. I wrote it on a sheet of paper with a diagram, to show how foetal circulation works before birth and after birth, what changes take place and in what sequence. I learned it almost by heart myself as I explained it to Dietrich. In the midweek exam we got the same question (how the foetal circulation works), so both of us knew well how to answer this question. When the results came, Dietrich's paper was marked 19/20 (she had one small error) and my paper was marked 13/20, which was a fail mark.

I took my exam paper to the tutor and asked her to show me where I was wrong. I told her that I had taught the sequence to Dietrich, that we learned it together, that she had been given the higher mark and I had been failed. She did not like me questioning the marking. Her reply was, "You are not supposed to check and compare papers!"

I am glad she was not the only tutor. We had a new tutor who came to lighten the load of the senior tutor. The deputy sister tutor was Miss Humphreys. She was God sent. We did benefit from her teaching as well as from the doctors' lectures. My grades were much higher with Miss Humphreys. I feared that sister tutor would fail me if she continued her grudge against me. I used to add up the exam results and then divide them to see if my average was a pass mark or a failure! I truly asked God to deliver me from the predicament I was in.

Most days sister tutor used to come into the classroom, sit at the edge of the table and tell us about the wartime stories that she had experienced. Before long the time was up and she was happy, but we were unhappy.

Nearer the end of the third year's training, she came and sat at the edge of the table as usual and started to tell us how many of us would pass our final exam. She hoped that we would all pass except me; then she openly said, "Ovsanna will fail." Then she came off her perch, went to the blackboard and wrote a very nasty word (I am glad my memory box did not harbour it). She added, "All Armenians are like (the bad word she had written on the blackboard)".

There were 15 nurses in the class. They all made a protesting noise. By this time I was crying with disgust. I hid my head in my arms and wished the earth would open and swallow me up. Then she said, "Miss Bedrossian, I would like to see you in my office after the class."

I had to leave the class first as usual because I sat in the first row. I stood at the threshold of the classroom door. As the nurses were passing me, they said, "Do not be afraid to speak out, we are on your side." I was not afraid, I was praying in tears, for it was God's time to act on my behalf.

The tutor went up into her office. I followed her, stood before her, and opened my heart to her, telling her: "I hope I can make myself clear to you with my broken English. I have not complained about you to the matron. I can not afford to lose six months, as I have already lost five years of nursing to gain the State Registered Nursing certificate from the KEM Hospital, in order to commence midwifery training."

I had been praying for two-and-a-half years since the incident about signing the exam application form. I hoped there might be reconciliation between tutor and student.

I was so devastated, physically trembling, expecting God to step in and deliver me from the situation. My prayers were heard.

Sister tutor had a sudden change of heart. These are the words that came from her mouth: "I am very sorry that as a teacher I have not gained your confidence in me. I will do this for you. I will give you some homework, that is to say five questions for you to answer; you can bring them back to me for correction." This was her way of trying to help me, but I only answered one question; I found it was diverting me from revising the rest of the subjects I had to learn.

Out of 15 students, only seven passed. I was one of them.

I will have to write how it all came to pass, simply to bring glory to the ever-present help from my Lord and Saviour. This will be in another chapter.

"When you pass through the waters, I will be with you; and when you pass through the rivers, they shall not sweep over you."

Isaiah 43:2

Harefields Hospital

As part of our nursing training, each nurse had to have three months of experience in a specialist hospital studying either psychiatric or pulmonary diseases. I was allocated to chest, heart and lung diseases. The Harefield had been used for decades for the treatment of patients with tuberculosis but, because of the decline of the disease, it was mostly used for cardiac and pulmonary surgeries.

Harefield Hospital was surrounded by beautiful gardens, open-air views and pleasant fields for walking, away from the noise and traffic of the busy town. To me it was a time of 'upper room' experience. We were to work day shifts the first six months and the rest on night shift. During the day shift I got to know Nurse Margaret Pitchford. She was the leader of the Nurses' Christian Fellowship. We had a very close friendship, which is still ongoing. The advantage of being away from the many obligations of living in town was being closer to God.

After a very busy night duty, we were in the breakfast room. Within me I seemed to hear a small voice saying, "Don't go to your night nurses' hut, wait until the post is delivered, then go." I began to take notice of this impulse and waited for the post to be delivered. But all the time my mind was saying, "You have never had a letter from your home, they are not letter writers." Nevertheless I obeyed this inner voice, and when the post was delivered there was a letter for me from Auntie Vergine. I knew that letter was important because it was supported by prayers from home. I walked through the field to my hut (the night nurses' dormitory was referred to as a hut) and when I got into my bedroom I closed the door and spread the letter before the Lord, and prayed for guidance on how to answer.

Mrs Vergine Badeer had received a letter from a relative called John who lived in Matlock, Derbyshire, telling them that his mother had wished him to marry an Armenian girl (John's mother had died some time before this letter was written.) They did not ignore this as being far-fetched – rather the whole clan prayed about it.

The Badeer family's custom was to come together each morning to read a short passage from the Bible, pray and ask God to lead them through the day. One day at this gathering they had read the contents of John's letter. John had lost his dad and a few years later his very dear mother had also died.

With the loss of his mother John was utterly devastated, because his mother had almost idolised him. He was the only child. His mother had craved for a child and after 18 years of marriage to Harold, a post office clerk, Mrs Sarah's desire had been met. John knew of nobody to whom he could turn for comfort, but his GP, Dr Dobson, who was very compassionate, had encouraged John to go with him in his car to some of the home visits, just to keep an eye on him.

The Badeer family, having prayed together, remembered

Left:
Hosanna (called 'Ovsanna' in her native Armenian tongue) came to know Christ at an early age.

Right:
After her graduation in 1958, Hosanna earned her white nurse's cap, a symbol of trust and responsibility.

...wifery training school at the Salvation Army Mothers' Hospital in Clapton, ...don, 1964-5 *(Hosanna is first right, on the front row).*

On 27th March, 1965, Hosanna and John were married at the Welsh church in Baker Street, London. Although only 15 people were expected for the ceremony and reception, on the day, more than a hundred people arrived to see the couple wed.

Shortly before the wedding, 'Goldie' the golden eagle famously escaped from London Zoo and spent nearly two weeks on the loose in Regent's Park. Hosanna wondered jokingly if some of her wedding guests had actually come to England in the hope of seeing Goldie!

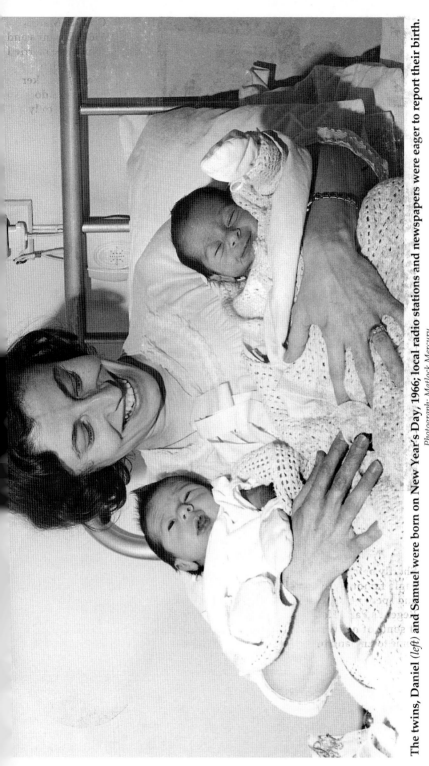

The twins, Daniel (*left*) and Samuel were born on New Year's Day, 1966; local radio stations and newspapers were eager to report their birth.

Photograph: Matlock Mercury

The Allen family at Christmas in 1980 (*left to right*) Paul, Daniel, Hosanna, John, Timothy and Samuel.

(*left to right*) Timothy, Daniel, Paul and Samuel at Broomfie... College, 19...

that Ovsanna, who had been one of their nurses in the CMC Hospital, was now in Ealing, London. They knew me very well from my childhood days and were also distantly related. They therefore put my name forward and asked Auntie Vergine to write me a letter, asking if I would be happy to give my address to John at Matlock. Then he would be able to get in touch with me and get to know me. The Badeers had absolutely no idea how old John might be.

Years before, when I was at the home of Dr Henry Badeer caring for their first-born son, Gilbert, I remembered hearing them once say that they had been given a Crown Derby teaset as a wedding present by relations who lived in Matlock, Derbyshire. I had been about nine to ten years old then.

After I read the letter sent to me by Auntie Vergine, I knelt by my bedside and spread the letter before the Lord and prayed: "Lord, the reason I came to England was to study to become a midwife, so that I might be able to go to the missionary field wherever the door opens for me." I had also promised Mr Vahan Postalian that I would not change my mind even if I met the right man to marry; that had been my reply to his challenge when I last met him before leaving Beirut.

"If it is God's will that I should marry, I would like to have a piano in my house to sing praises to His Name, and if He blesses me with children I will teach them about Jesus, and use my house for prayers." This was my prayer.

Following some consideration I answered Aunt Vergine's letter, giving her permission to give my address to John. In due course I received a letter from John, on an old piece of wartime letter paper. It was a fairly long introduction of himself, which did not interest me a bit. At the very end of the letter he wrote, "PS my hobby is to play the piano." This was the final piece of the jigsaw. I had prayed for a piano, should I have a home, to sing praises to His Name, teach choruses to my children and use the home as a house of prayer. When I read the PS, my attitude to marriage changed. I was filled with joy; I wanted to meet John. I wrote and asked him to come to London, so that we could meet.

That week I was not feeling well. When I saw the home

sister she had me X-rayed and admitted into the hospital nurses' sick bay. I was having chest pains and my temperature was up and down; but after a course of antibiotics and a few days of rest they allowed me to have a week off work. During this period Miss Alice Albarian and 20 others with her came from all over the Middle East for an educational tour.

An Armenian millionaire who had a share in the Arabian Gulf Oil Company arranged the three-month tour. He wanted to use his surplus money to help enhance the education system of the Armenian schools, colleges and universities. He paid all the expenses of these distinguished teachers from Syria and Lebanon. For three months they studied the education system of England and France to look at new methods of teaching technology which they could implement in their own schools, colleges and universities.

My sister-in-law, Miss Alice Albarian, wrote to tell me that she would be at the Hilton Hotel in London near Euston railway station for a week with another teacher called Janet (a relation).

The Harefield Hospital nursing officer had granted me a week's holiday. I used this opportunity to fix a date to meet with John at the St Pancras railway station. This was our first meeting. I put on my best winter dress which I had worn for my brother's wedding. I had John's name written on a piece of cardboard and waited for the train to arrive. He had written to say that he would be wearing an orange-coloured shirt.

I spotted him at first glance, no mistake. He was not what I had expected. I was talking with the Lord from inside my heart, "Lord, is this the boy you have for me from out of thousands? Could you not have chosen a better one?"

It was a great shock to see him as he presented himself to me – black tie, high heeled shoes pointed at the toes, black jacket with spots of glitter, orange-coloured shirt and a beige duffel coat.

We took a train to go somewhere. When a man sat near us, John kept looking at him and laughing. I was thinking, "He does not look any better to warrant his criticism of a fellow man." I was anxious to see him off as soon as possible.

When he checked the return train time and left, I was an unhappy person. I went to the Hilton Hotel to meet Miss Alice Albarian. They offered me a sandwich roll, but I could not eat.

For the first time in my life I had lost my appetite because of disappointment. I was crying inwardly. I was not only sorry for myself, but I also could not understand how a young adult could present himself to his first girlfriend in the way John had. Then I came to the conclusion that he was not my man. I would only help him through his bereavement period, and no further.

Near the end of Alice's stay in England they had a few more days before they had to travel to France. Alice and I decided to visit John. We both travelled to Matlock by train. When we arrived at the station hoping to see John he was not about, so we made our way to his house. I said to Alice as we approached the house, "The one facing us must be his house." We could tell from the torn curtains. We knocked at the front door, then the back door, but no one came. Eventually he opened the door. He was not feeling well, he had a cold.

The house was very cold, the floor was covered with newspapers, and the pieces of furniture in the two front rooms were almost stuck on top of each other. He had prepared a small tin of tomatoes on toast. We took our time eating and talked with him. I had made my mind up. He was not for me! I wanted to befriend him and be kind to him. We said goodbye and left.

John sent me his mother's picture with a dog sitting beside her, I sent him a pullover which I had knitted.

John's workplace was in Matlock Rail Station yard in a wooden office doing a clerk's job for British Railways. One day at lunchtime he met with Mr Potter, whose office was adjacent to John's. Mr Potter asked him if he went to church. He had no connection with any of the churches, so Mr Potter encouraged him to go to the Assemblies of God church at Jackson Road. They soon found out he could play the piano, so he started to play the piano at the AoG church. (He played there for 25 years.)

Another day John met Mrs Paterson face-to-face in the street. She stopped him and said, "You are my godson; when you were a baby we were friends with your parents." John did not know about this. From then on they showed him kindness by asking him for meals at the weekends and doing his washing every fortnight.

Shortly after we had started making friends with each other, she began to hint to John that this girl was after his house, and that he should stop communicating with me. John took her advice and wrote me a negative letter. I had a very bad letter from him, asking me to return the picture of his mother which he had given to me. I thought this was proof that he was changing his mind, so I gladly sent the picture back, and for nine months I did not reply to his letters. However, I did not stop praying, seeking God's will!

I shared this problem with close friends, wrote home asking for their prayers, for me to know God's plan for my life. No one was giving me sound wisdom, all I was hearing was, "We can't help you in this matter, you have to decide yourself."

I made up my mind to enquire of the Lord. I prayed and asked God to direct me with His wisdom and His Word. My natural thoughts were, "This is nothing but Satan's trick to divert me from my call to mission fieldwork." John's letters began slowing down. I had almost forgotten him and had to concentrate on my studies.

After months of silence, there arrived a desperate letter from John. He had tried asking one local lady to marry him, but he had been turned down. In his letter he sounded terribly downhearted; thoughts of harming himself if he were refused again were troubling him. This disturbed my spirit immensely.

Once again I clung to the Lord in my prayers. I recalled what I had heard in a lecture in psychiatric nursing – that we need to be aware of those who say or speak threatening words, that they tend to carry out their threat when they don't get their desires met! This was a time bomb. I took it very seriously and prayed. I started to examine myself, and hated to be the cause in any way of his depression.

Nevertheless, I was not going to make any decision unless I heard from the Lord, and knew within my heart whether it was the Lord's will or not. I meant business with the Lord.

Over three months I prayed, sought the Lord and tried going to different churches, hoping to hear God speak direct words of guidance.

I then seemed to have this compulsive thought to go to an Elim church where Dietrich had once taken me. One Sunday morning I put on my uniform, coat on top, took the bus and made my way to this Elim church where most of the congregation were young people. I thought to myself, these small churches usually don't end their services after an hour – they preach too long. If that happens, I will go without my Sunday lunch (alternate Sundays we had to work half a day, either morning or afternoon).

One spring Sunday morning I got to the Elim church by bus. The bus stopped right in front of the Elim church. I crossed the road. They had already started, so I entered and sat in the second row from the back. The church worship was lovely and alive, a good message, nothing particularly new.

I was pondering in my heart of hearts and communicating with the Lord as I would with a friend, saying to my Lord, "I listened to your prompting, and came all the way to this church, believing you are going to speak. I am here to listen, yes or no, regarding my reply to John's letter. I will not take any action unless you instruct me. Please, I really mean business, I need your help. Please help me."

Just as the pastor was about to announce the epilogue, there was this person who stood up in the middle of the congregation and started to speak in an unknown tongue. I was crying as I was reasoning with the Lord, "I came to hear your word and your instruction. The meeting is almost over and this person is speaking in a language I can't understand, even though I can understand five languages. Can't she say something that I may understand?" These words were still within my mind when, without any hesitation, the minister from the pulpit started interpreting the words that had been uttered. This is what I heard:

"I am the Lord your God, who brought you out of Egypt, your land, into this land upon the eagle's wings. I have

opened a wide door for you to enter. I am your Lord speaking to you. Fear not, I am the one bidding you to enter through this door, but you have been reluctant to enter. I, the Lord your God, who brought you upon the eagle's wings, am the one, bidding you to enter in. Fear not..."

(this was repeated three times)

I must mention here that a child sitting in front of me was coughing, so I was missing some of the things said by the interpreter. I was wishing that the child would stop coughing. At the end, I remember hearing the interpreter saying, "After you have suffered a little while, I shall settle you and establish you."

"The God of all grace, who called you to His eternal glory by Christ, after you have suffered a little while, will himself restore you and make you strong, firm and steadfast (settle you). *To Him be the power for ever and ever."*
1 Peter 5:10-11

This was it. I had heard the Lord speaking through the interpreter. I had never before had any such experience, but this was like a film showing my life. Because when I heard the minister say that He had brought me out of my mother's land into this strange land upon the eagle's wing, I knew these words were directly from the Lord to me – the airplane ticket that had been given to me had indeed been an eagle's wing. Secondly, when he said that God had opened a wide door and that I was reluctant to enter, I recognised that I was indeed reluctant to enter. Nothing could have changed my mind, except the Word of the Lord: "I am your Lord who is bidding you to enter and fear not!"

I was shedding tears of joy as I heard these words. I could face the future because it was God's bidding – "Fear not," and then the last verse he finished with, "I will settle you and establish you." The word 'settle' also was an indication, as in nursing, we are constantly changing rooms, in and out of the suitcases, day duty then night duty. Each time I used to repack my suitcase I used to say to myself, "How long, Lord, do I have to do this?" The prospect of having a home somehow meant the same to me as settling and being established.

I was on cloud nine through the large park towards the hospital, just in time for work at 1pm. I could hardly wait to get to my room to write the letter to John. I was going to accept, providing I was able to finish midwifery training.

The final seal of God's Word that day came when I was reading my New Testament passage for the day. It read, "After you have suffered a little while, (God) will Himself restore you and make you strong, firm and steadfast" (1 Peter 5:10).

Follow on

Down in the valley with my Saviour I would go, where the flowers are blooming and the sweet waters flow; everywhere He leads me I would follow, follow on, walking in His foot-steps till the crown be won.

Down in the valley with my Saviour I would go, where the storms are sweeping and the dark waters flow; with His hand to lead me I will never, never fear. Danger cannot frighten me if my Lord is near.

Down in the valley or upon the mountain steep, close beside my Saviour would my soul ever keep, He will lead me safely in the path that He has trod, up to where they gather on the hills of God.

Follow! Follow! I would follow Jesus;
Anywhere, everywhere, I would follow on!
Follow! Follow! I would follow Jesus;
Everywhere He leads me I would follow on!

William O Cushing, 1878

One morning at the hospital I was sitting on the steps in front of my bedroom door, reading my Bible and praying, pouring my heart's concerns out to the Lord. Something strange happened during my normal prayer; some strange words came out of my mouth. I stopped and questioned what it was. I had not consciously uttered these words, but the Holy Spirit was revealing the meaning of those couple of sounds unconsciously uttered by my mouth. But deep down within, my soul was crying, "Lord in reality, I would like to be a mother."

One day the Lord put it in my mind to find out how Margaret was doing at the Redcliffe Bible College in London. The best way of getting in touch with Margaret was to go to Westminster Chapel where Rev Doctor Martin Lloyd Jones used to hold Bible study sessions. Every Friday the chapel would fill with Bible school students. I thought, "That's what I will do." I took the underground train to St James underground station, the nearest to Westminster Chapel. I entered through the heavy wooden door on the right, found a seat and listened attentively to all that was being preached. When the meeting came to an end and everyone had left I stayed behind looking for Margaret. Finally I decided to leave. As I was coming out, down a few steps, a strong impulse told me to go back in. I stopped and thought, "What's the point of going in? There is no one left inside." Nevertheless, I obeyed my inner intuition and went in, this time through the high and heavy wooden door on the left.

To my great surprise Margaret was standing all on her own, right behind the door. I was so thrilled that I literally wrapped my arms around her screaming with joy and saying, "I have come especially to see you and find out how you were getting along since the sad occasion of your husband's death. I nearly missed seeing you. As I was coming down the steps, I heard this still small voice say, 'Go back in,' and after a moment of hesitation I obeyed, and I found you right behind the great heavy wooden door." I was astonished at how God works and gives us some surprises. She was as glad to see me as I was to see her. (God knew exactly where she was and sent me back in to find her.)

We both took the bus to Southhall. It was a double-decker

bus; we climbed to the top deck, sat at the back of the bus and Margaret told me all about what had happened since she had left the hospital.

Margaret's story

The grieving over her husband's death was having an effect on Margaret's studies. The college headmistress decided to have a talk with her, while 30 or so students were asked to pray for Margaret during her interview with the head of the college.

Margaret presented herself to the headmistress. After she had listened and been counselled, the headmistress asked her, "Have you prayed specifically for God to speak to you through His Word?"

Margaret left the office, went into her room feeling quite desperate and not knowing how and what to pray. She picked up her Bible and thumbed through it. As it opened at Isaiah 55:1-13, literally every verse came to her as a word from the Lord. Revelation is always the work of the Holy Spirit, who, by coming alongside us and opening the Scriptures to us, guides us into all truth. And when we go through such difficult times, when lack of understanding, confusion and lack of faith confront us, we need to bring those to the Lord, asking the Holy Spirit to make things clear to us. He will not let such prayers go unanswered.

Towards the end of my third year at KEM Hospital, I wanted to get in touch with Margaret. I visited her at her home and rang the front door bell. It took a few minutes for someone to open the door. As I was waiting I could hear laughter from the first floor of the house. Margaret had her friend with her and as soon as she opened the door, I could tell she was radiant with joy. Without my asking the reason for their laughter, she told me how she and her friend were practising changing car wheel skills without using an instruction book. This was in case she had a punctured tyre in the mission field, when it might not be possible to find a handyman in far-flung corners of the jungle of Sarawak in Borneo.

Margaret had accepted God's will for her life. She was fortified with the joy of knowing she was in the will of the

Lord, believing in and trusting the promises of God. She was prepared and ready to go to Borneo Mission. "The angel of the LORD encamps around those who fear Him, and He delivers them" (Psalm 34:7).

This was my last visit to Margaret's home. Soon after this she left for Borneo to work in Sarawak, all on her own. She kept in touch by writing exciting newsletters. I remember one of the first letters from her – she wrote that there were no dentists to be found, so she performed field surgery with a pair of pliers and extracted an infected tooth. This was a very courageous thing for her to do.

Practical State Final Exam

Miss Arpine Dombourian, an Armenian lady originally from Cyprus, played a big role in my coming to England. She was very able, witty, tall and attractive, with black curly hair. She spoke fluent English and was chosen to represent the King Edward Memorial Hospital on television. The hospital authorities were proud of her. She also had a very pleasant personality. Arpine sat her final exams six months before me. When the results were out, everyone was sad to hear she had failed.

When I heard about Arpine's failure it saddened me. All sorts of fears got hold of me, such as, "If such a clever nurse failed, then sister tutor must be right when she predicted that I would fail." I felt as though I were on stormy seas. I prayed and cast all my cares upon Him, for I knew He would see me through (1 Peter 5:7). As I was pondering sadly over Arpine's disappointment I came across Psalm 20:7: "Some trust in chariots and some in horses, but we trust in the Name of the LORD our God." How true this is. Arpine had great confidence in herself and did not study. This spurred me to take the exam very seriously and so I studied.

On the day of my written exam, I got up early in the morning, went to the park and spent some time praying, thanking and extolling the Name of Jesus, repeating the second portion of Psalm 20:7, "But I will trust in the Name of the Lord; when I call, He is right beside me to help."

A few weeks prior to my final practical exam I was sick

with a kidney infection, unable to eat or keep food down in my stomach, so I was hospitalised. My temperature was dangerously high. I was shivering (rigor) as though I was lying in a bed of snow, and vomiting violently. I was given an injection. The pain of that injection radiated right down to the tips of my toes. At night I became delirious. I wondered what sort of drug it was as only doctors were allowed to give this injection. I felt so ill, it felt as though I was being rotated on a carousel at high speed! I recall crying loudly like a child for my mother. A very close eye was kept on me, day and night. I was dehydrated, and the doctor threatened me, saying, "If you don't eat or drink, we shall put up a saline drip." Unknown to me, everyone had been told that I had a psychosomatic illness. But I knew it was not so because I had no fear of the exam; I had studied well and knew that I would pass.

After being given treatments such as an ice-cold blanket sponge bath to bring my temperature down, I reached out for my Bible and found the chapter I had come to. Isaiah 54:17 jumped up from the page: "'No weapon forged against you will prevail, and you will refute every tongue that accuses you. This is the heritage of the servants of the LORD, and this is their vindication from me,' declares the LORD." This was the best injection of faith I needed at that very time. Isn't the Lord good? He is on target in all His acts. (He had shut the mouth of the lions.)

I had a peaceful night's sleep.

Early next morning the home sister herself came to check my temperature. It had gone down. She could not believe it, so she shook the thermometer, put it back into my mouth, stayed with me a good few minutes, took the thermometer out of my mouth and read it. "No temperature," she said and went back to her desk. Home sister came back at 9am and checked my temperature. It was still down, so she asked me if I would like to go for my practical exam. Without hesitation I said, "Yes, please." She left the room to arrange transport for me.

This was the working of my God. I would like all those who read these true stories to see the way the Almighty God works, because He loves us and cares for His children. I do hope all the glory goes to Him.

That day I was treated like royalty. The matron's chauffeur was asked to take us to the examination centre. The nurse who had to take repeat exams was appointed to take care of me both ways. Before we left, home sister gave me two tablets to swallow, to make sure my temperature stayed down. We boarded the private taxi and drove to the exam centre in London.

When we arrived at the centre, they were expecting us. There was no hanging about. I was taken to a lounge, given a nice hot cup of tea and asked if I was feeling all right. Yes, I was ready. The nurse who had accompanied me opened the next door, introduced me and left.

I was asked to set up two trolleys: one for spinal puncture and the other as an orthopaedic traction trolley. I set them quickly and confidently. I was asked several questions: What do we do? Why do we do this? What are the dangers? And many more such questions. It took hours. As soon as I had finished, the examiner said, "You have passed."

We were driven back to hospital and I was taken back to the sick bay. I had already sat my written exam prior to being sick. On my return from the exam, the matron had received a crate full of Lucozade bottles. She brought them all to the sick bay for nurses to drink, and I attribute my recovery to those pints of Lucozade; I was discharged after a week with no temperature.

My next duty was in the out-patients department, in the varicose vein treatment clinic. It was my duty to set up the trolley for these treatments. One day, I put out the necessary dressings on the trolley, went to check something, and when I came back to help the doctor I found that what I had placed on the trolley had been tampered with.

I could hear some of the nurses from my class talking about me behind my back. They were in the urine-testing cubical and I knew they had moved the sterile dressings to the bottom of the trolley to see what I would do. They were real bullies.

This was the day when our final exam results were to be given out. After being bullied while I was working in outpatients department my classmates were also shouting, "Nurse Bedrossian, do you think you will pass?" I did not answer any of their questions, as they were trying to make me cry. "In quietness and trust is your strength" (Isaiah 30:15). This was what I was meditating.

Before lunch I was called to the matron's office. The senior tutor was sitting next to the matron. Matron opened the brown envelopes and read the first line, "I have the pleasure of informing you that you have passed." As soon as she read the word 'pleasure', sister tutor took over and began to congratulate me. We shook hands and I thanked sister tutor in front of the matron. I did not show any emotion, but walked out and went back to outpatients department to finish what I had been doing.

There the girls in my class were all looking at me with wide eyes. Here too I did not show any emotion, and I left them to find out for themselves whether I had passed or failed. Inwardly, however, I was rejoicing and thanking the Lord for being at my right hand. (Out of 15 nurses, seven had passed, including me.)

I wrote to John to tell him the good news. He had already agreed that I should do the midwifery training I had come to do in England. John came to see me, this time to buy the engagement ring. I went to meet him. We went and bought the ring, walked to the end of the street and he put the ring onto my left hand. He already had a ring on his right hand. Now I was engaged to John, relying on the interpretation of the prophecy given in the Elim church at Ealing. I would become Mrs Hosanna Allen (Hosanna is the English translation of Ovsanna).

By this time, I had already applied for midwifery training and I was accepted at the Salvation Army Mothers' Hospital at Clapton, East London. I left the KEM Hospital and joined the Mothers' Hospital at the end of September, 1963.

There was one undone thing which was uppermost in my mind and that was that I had not been faithful in my tithing to the Church. I prayed, asking the Lord where to send this sum of money. For three years the hospital had given us £20 pocket money every month. I used to send some of it to my mother. This time I seriously prayed about where to give my tithes. I had attended so many churches in the Ealing district but I did not belong to any of them. After much prayer and waiting, the Scriptures that kept coming to mind convinced me.

> *"'Bring the whole tithe into the storehouse, that there may be food in my house. Test me in this,' says the LORD Almighty, 'and see if I will not throw open the floodgates of heaven and pour out so much blessing that you will not have room enough for it.'"*
>
> (Malachi 3:10)

I was pondering which mission to send the money to. None of them seemed right. I had clearly forgotten about Margaret Broadly going to the Borneo mission in the Far East. One day it flashed through my mind that Margaret had gone to the Borneo Mission. As soon as this thought burst into my mind, I knew that this was it. Peace of mind surrounded me and I had no doubt. I went to the bank and asked the bank clerk, "Please, could you send ten percent of what there is in my account to this address in Borneo?"

He was surprised and said, "I have never had such a request before. Are you sure?"

I replied, "Yes, quite sure, thank you and goodbye."

Within ten days or so I received a letter from Borneo. Margaret had received the sum and was thanking me. This is what she had written: "I was praying this morning, expressing my desire to take part in the European Mission conference taking place on an island near Borneo, but had no money to attend. I came off my knees and went to see if there were any letters. Your envelope had arrived just in time, so I was able to be at the conference." I was so glad to have been obedient to God's bidding. This was the happiest day of my life, reading the contents of Margaret's letter.

Midwifery training at Salvation Army Mothers' Hospital in Clapton

At the end of September new students were to come, so we had to leave our rooms. I was glad the day had arrived for me to transfer to the Salvation Army Mothers' Hospital at Clapton.

We were warmly welcomed, taken to our rooms and shown round the hospital. The following day started with 15 minutes of assembly. There was so much life and respect towards everyone, a pleasant atmosphere in all the wards, unity amongst staff and tutors. To sum it up, for me it was like twelve months of holidays. We worked very hard, doing overtime most of the time, but it was pleasant to see new life and rejoicing mothers and fathers.

One significant activity was after each baby was born. The mother and baby were washed and made comfortable. The nurse who had delivered the baby first wrote the report with details of the time, weight, any abnormality etc. Then she would let the mother cuddle the baby. The nurse would ask if the mother would like the nurse to thank the Lord for a new life and for safe delivery of the baby. This created a good bond between the mother and baby, as well as between the midwife and mother.

We used to get a number of unmarried mothers, who were well looked after and ministered to by the Salvation Army social services.

There were ten of us in my class. After six months of study, together with practical work, we all got good results. One day sister tutor was looking for me to impart the good news that I had done well and was second in the top grade. I thoroughly enjoyed my whole year at the Mothers' Hospital, learned fast, spiritually too. We were fed from the sound Word of the Scriptures through the able-bodied Salvation Army officers and we attended their activities throughout the year.

After six months of theory and practice within the hospital, we had to have six months of district midwifery, so we needed some form of transport. Most of the nurses could cycle except me. One of my friends volunteered to teach me to cycle. We went to the riverside near the park. I was helped onto her bicycle and I tried to balance myself, but unfortunately I fell and hurt my wrist. I tried to put on a brave face, got back on the bicycle, hoping this time I would be able to balance myself. Yet again I failed to master the art of cycling. We decided to call it a day and went home. After supper, I went to bed to rest and sleep. Somehow my wrist was getting increasingly painful and began to swell. It kept me awake all night.

The following day I reported the incident to the home sister. My wrist was X-rayed and it showed that I had a fractured bone. It was put in a plaster cast and had to stay in plaster for six weeks. This was the beginning of my district midwifery – my right hand in plaster. Normally I am left-handed, but I had been made to write with my right hand, so I was not much good in the district.

My first call-out was in the Shoreditch area of East London. A senior midwife had to go with me in any case, to teach me the home procedures for delivery. The home where the birth was to take place was on the third floor. All the necessary precautions and preparations were already in place as it was the mother's fourth pregnancy. It was expected to be a fairly normal birth but after a few hours it was proving to be a difficult one, so the midwife called an ambulance. The lady was given pain relief and was swiftly transferred to hospital. The baby was in the breech position, so everyone was happy when the baby was delivered safely shortly after the mother had arrived at the hospital. I was more than pleased that the birth had taken place in hospital because I could not have been much help with my painful wrist.

Even in this I could see God's deliverance in time of need.

Regarding Auntie Berth

Auntie Berth Pelling was first introduced to me by a Swiss sister called Miss Ruth Okes, who had come from Switzerland to Beirut in Lebanon to take the position of matron at the Christian Medical Centre where I was working. When she had heard that I was preparing to go to England to study nursing further, she had given me the address of Mrs Pelling in London. Ruth had asked me to meet with Berth and had given me an oriental tablecloth to give to her as a present from Lebanon.

When I arrived in London I sent this gift of a tablecloth to Berth's address. I soon had a reply telling me that Berth had received the parcel. She also warmly welcomed me in her letter. Later she came to see me in KEM Hospital and we took to each other. She was such a warm-hearted, hospitable middle-aged lady, newly married to Mr Pelling who had been a prisoner of war in Japan. He had suffered at the hands of the Japanese Army and had had tuberculosis. When he returned to his country no one would associate with him. However, he was glad to have met Berth, who was a good cook and had a pleasant personality. They both helped to clean the Swiss church in London, and occasionally I joined in helping them, so we had fellowship with each other.

Berth was so sincere and loving, I felt welcome in their home any time I felt alone and needed their hospitality. Berth also suggested that I could go to Switzerland during my long annual holiday. So this dream came true – and she even gave me French lessons.

I decided to take up their offer to go to Switzerland for a fortnight in June 1962. I got all the necessary papers, passport, ticket etc. I was looking forward to this journey. Halfway through the channel crossing, our passports had to be checked. When it was my turn I showed my passport and the officer took it from me. Then there was some conversation between the officers. Before long they called me into a confined area, abandoned me in this prison room, locked the door and left. Suddenly it dawned on me that I was imprisoned. There was a tiny window through which passengers were looking in and whispering to each other. I was in great fear and cried uncontrollably.

Thank goodness they returned, got me out, took me to the deck and tried to explain that without a French visa I was not allowed to cross through France to get to Switzerland. They said that they had the authority to send me back to England. I prayed and the answer came within a few minutes.

They came back with a letter attached to my passport and advised me to see an officer at the French border. I had to follow the address on my passport, pay £15 and have the passport stamped before I could travel to Switzerland. I had learned a lesson. It was no good telling them that I did not know that I should have had a visa for all the countries I intended to pass through.

I arrived safely at Lausanne station, where Miss Anne Zuolph and Miss Okes were waiting. Ruth Okes took me to her home and I had a much-needed bubble bath and restful night's sleep. The following day I was instructed to take the train to Champanyon village. I had a fantastic holiday. The three Swiss sisters whom I knew from the Christian Medical Centre in Beirut took it in turns to entertain me while I was in Switzerland.

7

Looking ahead to the day of the wedding

There was excitement in the air; the door was about to open, as had been promised by the Lord once the path was cleared. The date of the wedding was fixed and the invitation cards were distributed. Neither of us knew where to begin, but God knew every detail because He had heard me asking for His help, especially when John told me in no uncertain way, that it was the bride's family who were responsible for the wedding expenses. This was contrary to the Middle Eastern tradition. When I read the information from a magazine cutting which John posted to me, I understood why John told me so. The best thing I could do was to bring all my anxieties to Jesus and leave them at his feet.

> *"Cast all your anxiety on Him because He cares for you."*
> 1 Peter 5:7

> *"Do not be anxious about anything, but in everything, by prayer and petition, with thanksgiving, present your requests to God. And the peace of God, which transcends all understanding, will guard your hearts and your minds in Christ Jesus."*
>
> Philippians 4:6-7

Mrs Manoushag, the widowed lady who lived in Ealing in the same building as the triplets, had a daughter who had married Dr Charles McLean. They lived in Repton in Derbyshire. Auntie Manoushag knew me well. She had told her son-in-law, Dr Charles, about me and he was intrigued with the story that Manoushag had told them. Dr Charles and his wife wished to meet me in person; they asked me in a letter to pay them a visit in Repton. I visited them as arranged. I was asked many questions and I replied to all their questions satisfactorily. After a prayer they saw me off at the train station in Derby. I travelled back to Clapton.

While I was in Repton with the McLeans I mentioned that, once the twelve months of training were over, all the midwives had to leave the hospital so that the new recruits could be accommodated in our place. The wedding date was six weeks later, but at some point during that six-week period the students would have to sit their State Registration final exam. Once the final date for this exam was announced, all the students would have to find their way to the exam centre in London.

In due course I received a letter from Dr McLean, inviting me to spend the six weeks in their house at Repton. He suggested that he and his wife would be very glad to help me in any way they could. He would drive the three of us, once a week, to John's house 20 miles away in Matlock, so that we could clean the house, put up new curtains and sort out the 'Aladdin's Cave' for the bride and groom.

Dr McLean was a retired missionary who had worked for many years in Jordan. He was one of the main founders of the Faith Hospital establishment, which is still in operation under the government of King Hussein's son. Mrs Lucien McLean had been invited to its grand opening and had received a signed picture of King Hussein, which she treasures.

Following the doctor's letter, I received another invitation from an unexpected source. This was from Mrs Arshag Raffie of Paddington in London. She wrote, "I have just come across your wedding invitation. I had put it in one of my Bibles and forgotten it. I would dearly love to be of any help to you during your wedding period. I suggest you come with your bridesmaid to stay with me in my house. We will prepare a party for your guest of honour and you could get dressed in your wedding gown on the day. I will even arrange for the cars to take you to the Welsh church in Baker Street, near Madam Tussauds." What else could I wish for?

How did I get to know Auntie Arshag Raffie? She was the daughter-in-law of a famous Armenian poet. The manuscripts of his poems represent the richness of Armenian culture; these books were kept in the Armenian church.

However, whenever Rev Samuel Doctorian came to England, he used to stay in her home and receive her hospitality. Since the death of her husband, however, Rev Samuel used to stay elsewhere. Rev Samuel was preaching in the Metropolitan Tabernacle where Spurgeon had preached in London. The preacher used to draw people from all walks of life. The auditorium was full to overflowing. My friends and I, twelve of us in all, had come to hear Rev Samuel. After a very inspiring message he gave an altar call. Many went forward and knelt, including me. He laid hands on each one and prayed. When he came to me, he did not touch my head, only held his hand over and as he was praying I felt a powerful current passing through me. When I stood to go to my seat I could hardly walk. I hid myself behind a pillar, praying with tears of joy. Later Mrs Arshag came and whispered in my ear, "When you were touched by the Holy Spirit's power, at that moment something happened to me too." From that day on we were spiritual friends.

The wedding gown

I had a friend named Mary, an Armenian, originally from Brazil. She had come to London in search of work or to do nursing. She had married a few years earlier. Her wedding gown had cost 19 guineas when she bought it new. Though she had sold it to her friend, she was sure she could ask for it back, so that I could borrow it for a week for my wedding day. Three days before the wedding I was invited with my bridesmaid to go and stay at Auntie Arshag's house.

Mary had asked us to go and fetch the wedding gown from her home. She had reclaimed the gown with all its contents from its second owner. We collected the box from Mary's house, a large white oblong box with all the essential items in it – the veil, tiara, shoes, stockings, everything, including a New Testament from Jerusalem with a mother-of-pearl cover.

It needed two of us to carry the box through the busy underground stations to Paddington where I was staying. In the morning Auntie Arshag spread a large white sheet on the floor in the middle of the lounge and set up an ironing board with an iron. She said, "You have all day to iron the gown," and left for work.

The following day Auntie Arshag took the wedding veil and coronet, wrapped them in a white linen sheet and carried them held high in the air through the busy streets of Paddington into the hairdresser's salon. She said, "This is the lady who is to wear the veil and coronet. Her hair is thin, so make sure the coronet stays on her head without moving or falling during the wedding ceremony." I was staggered at the extent of the care and love she put into making the day enjoyable.

On the last night before the wedding we had our baths, went to bed to sleep and rest for a busy day ahead. Being a light sleeper, I woke up very early and smelt burning. I ran down the steps with fear in my heart thinking, "It can't be happening, is the house on fire?" I rushed down from the third floor to the basement to find out what was happening, but to my great surprise there was Auntie Arshag cooking not just for my guests' lunch, but also for the wedding reception. I was deeply touched by her huge sacrifice, her action was so praiseworthy. She would not let me help her; instead, she sent me back to bed.

Regarding the photographer

The triplets' mother knew of a retired gentleman, newly arrived in London from Cyprus. When he heard of this wedding of the year, he offered of his own free will to come and take pictures of the wedding. He took 40 black-and-white pictures, enlarged them, and gave them to us as a present.

About the flowers

Auntie Berth's husband, Mr Pelling, knew a certain Mr Jacob who worked in Kew. He was the superintendent of Kew Gardens. These two were good friends. When Mr Jacob heard about this lonely girl's wedding, which was to take place at the Welsh church in Baker Street, he went with Mr Harry to find out about the colour scheme of the church. He then wanted to decorate the church with suitably-coloured flowers, arrange the buttonholes etc. God took care of the flower colour scheme too. What a God we have!

On Friday all the members of the wedding party were in London, as advised by Pastor Steven Wang, to have a rehearsal of the ceremony. We met with the church caretaker, who was asked to take orders from us as to how many bottles of milk we would need. I had told him days before that we were going to be about 10 or 15 people at the most and that we needed three bottles of milk for cups of tea at the reception. It was going to be a very humble reception, with sandwiches, tea and cake.

John had chosen his distant cousin to act as his best man, John Poladian, a businessman living in London, who had emigrated from Cyprus. Doctor McLean was to give me away, the triplets were to be junior bridesmaids, their brother Vartan would be page-boy and Poladian's niece would be the senior bridesmaid.

Auntie Berth had made a large wedding cake. There was another wedding cake – I think the second one was from 15 nurses. Mrs Lucien also baked various confectioneries for the reception while I was in Repton.

Dr McLean and Lucien used to spend their holiday in Paris every year. Dr Charles had a map of Paris showing hotels and tourist places of interest in the centre, such as the Eiffel Tower, theatres and so on. He had passed it on to John so John had arranged and planned all the places we were intending to see each day. The newly-weds were to stay in a hotel the first night. The following morning we had to travel by train and ferry boat to spend our honeymoon in Paris. We had British Railway privilege free tickets, but John had to pay for the hotel and meals.

The three Swiss nursing tutors with whom I had worked in Beirut CMC hospital came prepared to contribute their musical talents. They were the main entertainers. (These three ladies had met me when I spent my annual holiday in Switzerland the previous year.) When they received my invitation, they decided to come for a week's holiday, thinking this was their opportunity to visit England for the first time. The day of the wedding we were busy preparing the church and the reception. They arrived to give us a hand, which we badly needed. We went and bought more bottles of milk and light beverages for the reception as the numbers were swelling. In all, 100 people, nearly everyone who had received an invitation, replied saying they were coming.

Pastor Oswald Potter came with his wife and daughter from Matlock.

At the same time as all of this was going on, the famous golden eagle of London Zoo had broken loose from the confined area of its sheltered zoo and was roaming in Regent's Park. It was the world news of the century, people from all over were eager to see this runaway golden eagle. The public were being entertained by this novelty.

Every single need was met and the tangible presence of Jesus was felt at this wedding, turning water into wine. A card from my home carried the same message!

The message Pastor Wang gave was also about Jesus turning water into wine. His Spirit was permeating the atmosphere, His presence was tangible, and Jesus was the host. I want to give Him all the praise. There were several telegram messages and gifts, some of them still not opened. I believe all those who gave were also blessed – it is by giving that we receive, this is God's principle.

Dear reader, I am no different from you; what He has done for me, He is longing to bless you also, believe in God. Trust in Him.

> *"Delight yourself in the* Lord *and He will give you the desires of your heart. Commit your way to the* Lord; *trust in Him and He will do this..."*
>
> (Psalm 37:4-5)

Regarding John

Bewildered John needed help and advice after his long and painful bereavement. After losing both parents in the space of two years, he was not prepared for such a change. He had no domestic skills, simply because Mother had spoiled him and almost idolised him since his early childhood. John wished to do things, but his beloved mother overprotected him, because Mother had had him late in her life after waiting for 17 long years. His dad had not been keen to have children, but Mother dearly loved to mother children. When eventually God granted her heart's desire, the outcome was disastrous! Dad was too old, set in his ways and had different hobbies, one of which was to spend all his spare time at the auctions. He would buy and stack the items in his four-bedroom house. Mother's hobby was to cook and make preserves from the apples harvested from the garden. She was skilful in wine-making and also in embroidery.

John had had a very sheltered life. He had not been allowed to play with other children in case he got hurt; his eating habits were also peculiar compared with those of others of his age. He was so intertwined with his mother that even now his mother is never far from his thoughts. No one could fill that emptiness in his heart and mind. I prayed that God would take that place in his heart. John has a unique complicated character, slow but sure, clean but with lots of phobias. He has a keen musical ear, a keen memory, and a one-track mind. He is God's choice for me, I have come to accept his ways and I love him with the love of the Lord. I thank God for him.

Turning a house into a home

When I was a very young child we had a tiny washroom. I imagined that if I had the same size room I would place my bed in one corner, put a table and a chair beside it, with a lamp on the table, a jug of water and a pot of macaroni with mince meat! That's all I asked of the Lord. That would have satisfied me in my life!

Who would have thought that 20 years later I would be engaged with cleaning a house full of earthly possessions, some items for the fire, some for general auction, some to give away, some for the rubbish bin, some to save for their potential usefulness, yet some to be taken to Sotheby's to sell.

While I was staying at the McLeans' house during the six-week period before the wedding, Dr Charles drove the three of us 20 miles from Repton to Matlock, to prepare the house John had lived in all his life, for his bride.

The house is centrally situated and enjoys a private position with picturesque views. It is conveniently situated near all the town amenities. The railway and other public transport, the Derwent River and Hall Leys Park are all within walking distance.

When we got in the house it felt cold, draughty and damp because the fireplaces in all the rooms had been left open and the floors had a layer of lino on top of wooden flooring. There was no electricity except in the back kitchen. There was one electric bulb, an old gas stove in the kitchen with frying pans, not only greasy, but worn with holes that leaked. There were several bulky Chesterfield armchairs, some stacked on top of one another, a twelve-seater heavy dining room table, a grand piano, large tall bookcases almost touching the ceiling, two walnut sideboards, one ten foot long and the other eight foot long, a billiard table, a beautiful Queen Mary model boat in a glass case and eight encyclopædias, never opened, still in their corrugated wrapping.

However, the three of us came once a week while John was at work in Derby to do a major clear-out. Some days Pastor Potter came and sorted some of the woollen underwear to give to an old people's home. Mrs Patterson collected all the embroidery cottons. Auntie Lucien made the lampshades and the curtains for the front rooms.

John had already had the rewiring and papering of the walls done professionally. The only fireplace in use was in the back kitchen. But after much cleaning, the house became liveable.

After coming back from the honeymoon, I spent months cleaning areas that had never been cleaned before, my hands were black after washing. To hide them I wore gloves whenever I went to church.

New beginning

Having had a memorable honeymoon in Paris, we arrived home with much anticipation to strengthen each other and fulfil our ambition of establishing a warm loving home. My dream of a settled life had begun. We committed ourselves each day to His will. There was much to learn – preparing meals for my husband and keeping the house clean and warm. To do this it was necessary for me to cut some hardboard to size and use it to cover all the fireplaces to stop the draughts. Some of the rooms were still cluttered with items no longer required; however, they were valuable enough to sell and use the proceeds to have central heating installed. This we did.

The clearing of every crack and cranny continued. There was so much to keep me occupied. I enjoyed all the spring-cleaning, going through the drawers, shelves, thousands of books, eight encyclopædias and a trunk full of carpentry tools, all new, neatly packed in layers of rustproof papers.

One day I was tidying the Singer sewing machine set by the bay window, covered in dust and rusting. It had four drawers. I found needles, thimbles, coloured bobbins of cotton, crochet hooks, scissors, etc… enough to last me for the years to come. Suddenly the Holy Spirit nudged me, implying, "You don't need to worry for anything." (You did not pray for such small useful items, but I was mindful of your smallest needs.) I was overwhelmed with my Lord's generosity towards me. I wept with gratitude in my heart. To think the Lord had gone before me, supplying ALL my needs.

> *"And my God will meet all your need according to His glorious riches by Christ Jesus."*
>
> Philippians 4:19

Soon after our marriage John was made redundant. The Matlock office was pulled down and he was temporarily posted to Rowsley Station. We both attended the Assemblies of God church, where John played the piano on Sundays. At the weekends we visited friends, had lovely walks along the River Derwent and did some gardening.

We were expecting our first child in mid January. We prepared for the arrival of the new baby. I prepared all the necessary provisions for John during my absence, including sacks of coal stacked in the coalhouse. I did not leave anything undone. At 11pm I could hardly walk up the steps, when two sparrows came in from the attic window, chirping away. I talked to them and wondered what they were trying to say. I had hardly got into bed when the alarms of labour pains started, two weeks before the expected date.

The birth of unexpected twin baby boys

At 8am on New Year's Day, 1966, at Darley Dale maternity wing, I was taken into the labour room. The doctor was called and the baby was born. While the doctor was wearing his gloves, the nurse was trying to take a blood sample from the baby's umbilical cord; but the blood was not running into the test tube. The doctor suspected there must be another heartbeat and asked the nurse to listen for another heartbeat.

"Yes, there's another heartbeat," the nurse announced to my delight.

Towards the end of my pregnancy I had suspected that I might be carrying twins because I could feel two lumps. I loved watching twins. There had been a pair at our school. They had always captured my attention as they walked past. I used to admire their graceful likeness. My mother, too, had had twin girls when I was three years old. Unfortunately they both died at nine months from a tummy infection called 'summer diarrhoea'.

My sister had once told me, "We are not likely to have twins, because it runs in every alternate generation." I am glad she was wrong. God knew my deepest desire and He met it. I was blessed beyond my expectation. Later I was called in to the doctor's office. He seemed apologetic, thinking I was crying because I had not been prepared for twins. No, on the contrary, I was crying with deep gratitude, saying to the Lord "I am not worthy of these gifts of life entrusted into my care." It's so beautiful to feel blessed by the Almighty giver of love and life.

Incidentally, we had only thought of a girl's name. Now I was confronted with the question of what to call the identical twin boys. The only names coming to my mind were Daniel and Samuel. John was not with me to help me decide.

While I was in the labour room and the first baby had just been born, the telephones were ringing from Derby, Chester-field and Sheffield, asking the midwife for any New Year's Day births in hospitals so that they could be announced in their newspapers. I remember hearing the nurse saying, "Hold on, not quite over; could you hold the line please? We think it's twins; hold on, we will soon know the gender!"

Obviously the newspapers heralded the news in the sur-rounding towns. In due course, I received a letter from a lady in Nottinghamshire asking, "If your twins were like mine, un-expected, I have good news for you. We have a twin pram in our corridor. If you need it, come and collect it, for a small fee."

Doctors Charles and Lucien came to see the twins. They were delighted to see the babes. I told Dr Charles, "You gave away Lucy Armenagian (the mother of the triplets). She had triplets. Then you gave me away, and I had twins. I strongly recommend you to give brides away so that they can have multiple births!"

Doctors Charles and Lucien went and fetched the twin pram. It served as a crib for the first few months. It has just occurred to me that maybe the two sparrows flying into the house from the attic the night before were God's way of declaring two new lives.

First visit to Beirut with the twins

Five years had swiftly passed since my arrival in England. I was longing to go back home and tell them how good the Lord had been in leading me. But before leaving home, I had something important to tell Lucien. Although I had been on contraceptive pills I was feeling sickly in the mornings and had already missed a period.

Rev Lazarian was still helping Rev Samuel Doctorian at the School of Life and in the orphanage run by the church community.

I was honoured to declare the Name of Jesus amongst my school friends, church ladies' groups, neighbours and acquaintances. "Give thanks to the LORD, call on His Name; make known among the nations what He has done" (Psalm 105:1). He had done great things whereof we were glad.

The money that was tithed, plus child allowance (for the second child only in those days), paid for my journey to Beirut. My dad was so pleased to see his grandsons, as he had lost his twin baby girls plus another baby girl in their infancy. It was a profitable visit. We were all pleased to see each other. It was very hard to leave them behind. We said our goodbyes and I boarded the airplane.

Incidentally, on my way back, I missed the air connection at Heathrow Airport. Fortunately there was another flight for Manchester two hours later. I was only sorry for Dr Charles, as they had to meet me at Manchester airport to bring us home. They graciously waited till we arrived and drove us to Matlock, then they drove to their home at Repton.

While on holiday I went with my sister and her family to visit Rev Vahram. His eldest son had been one of the fatalities in the bus crash of summer 1960, when the school lost 24 of its pupils. The church congregation had been split and it had left many broken hearts. Rev Vahram had been most severely affected by this and was suffering with stress. He asked me to which church I was connected. I said, "AoG," which he did not appreciate. That night I could not sleep with worrying about whether I was going to the wrong church. My brother-in-law was in the balcony that night, I asked him what he thought of the AoG church when he came to Matlock to visit us a year before. He said he had been very pleased with what he saw and heard, he experienced the Lord's presence in the church. I said, "But Rev Vahran does not approve." He then said, "I should not worry, you follow God's direction."

I was right in my suspicion – nine months later Timothy Emmanuel was born. Auntie Gloria took care of the twins during my week in the maternity ward. The six-day war between the Arabs and Israelis ended and the Jews got back the Wailing Wall. 'Puppet on a string' was heard all over the air.

After the twins and Timothy started school, I began looking for a job. Social Services were pleased to employ me.

Interpretation of prophecy

John's redundancy was weighing heavily on my mind. One Thursday I wrote a letter expressing my discontent to nursing friends in the USA to see if I could find a job in America. I gave several reasons why I was taking this decision. I sent copies of the letter to most of the friends I had abroad. John came home from work and had his supper. I put the children to bed and went to a prayer meeting.

Half way through the prayers, a lady spoke in tongues, spontaneously Pastor Potter interpreted the message. It was so clear, I believed the message was directed at me, as no one ever knew what I had done that day. God must have been watching me write that letter. This was the interpretation: "You have been looking for salvation at other shores; your salvation is on your doorstep." I was sobbing with tears of discontent. What would I do when my husband became jobless? My argument with the Lord turned to submission. I said to the Lord through my tears, "If this is you telling me that my salvation is on my doorstep, I believe you; now please prove yourself."

The house had no doorbell at the time. I decided that the next day I would make it my priority to buy a doorbell from Woolworths and try to fix it as best I could. First thing in the morning I dressed the children, put them in the pushchair, went to buy the doorbell and fixed it. The same bell is still in operation 38 years later and, each time it rings, I expect a blessing, not only for myself, but also for those who come to my threshold. I desire to do them good. I do sincerely pray this blessing to continue, for His glory. I keep myself occupied with providing Bed and Breakfast for students. My hobbies are painting and embroidery.

Mrs Valerie and I had met in the maternity ward at Darley Dale. She had had a baby girl on Christmas Day and I had given birth to the twins on New Year's day. The local newspaper had put us in the news with our pictures.

Six months later Valerie came to visit us. She brought her

beautiful baby girl, Elizabeth. I took her upstairs and showed her the third bedroom, emptied of all its furniture, walls painted, with two new beds for the twins to use when they had grown. Valerie said, "I am receiving Bed and Breakfast overflow from guesthouses. When I receive more visitors, I will send my overflow to you." But I said, "I don't know how to cook English breakfast." She told me what she did and shortly after this friendly visit I had a couple come with their ten-year-old son. They had been sent by Valerie and needed accommodation.

As they stood at the door, I told them that my twins cried and made a noise at night. "I fear they might disturb your sleep."

"Oh, no! Don't worry, we are a family, that does not bother us." They were invited in, taken into their room, shown around, made to feel at home.

The following morning they said they had slept well and enjoyed their breakfast. The lady came to the kitchen and said, "We like Matlock very much and would like to stay another night. Could you put us up?"

I replied, "By all means, yes." I went behind the kitchen door and jumped up and down with joy, thanking the Lord. The following day, they again requested to stay another night. I went behind the door and thanked the Lord for His provision. They extended their stay by three days. I needed this provision for that week because on Monday the milkman had asked me for milk money owing for three weeks. After I had paid him, I was left with seven shillings.

The timing of this incident was due to a desire to give my testimony to young Sunday school girls between the ages of seven and twelve years. Pastor Potter had asked volunteers to help in the Sunday school. I went a few times to help when my mother was with us (she had come to see us from Beirut). She looked after my boys while I was at the Sunday school. I wanted to invite the girls to my home, give my testimony and offer them ice cream; but on Monday when the milkman came and asked for three weeks' unpaid milk money I was left with seven shillings. I did not have enough money left to buy ice cream. I quickly knelt at the kitchen settee and said to the Lord, "Lord, I wish to give the girls ice cream, I am not good at making ice cream at home. If I could offer Walls ice cream from the shop, it would be best." (The seven shillings would also have to buy us bread and food until I got money from my husband, John.)

On the Thursday after breakfast, when our lady visitor was paying, I could not keep my joy to myself. I told her how her extended stay was meeting a need and that it was an answer to a prayer. She was glad to hear this and said, "I am glad you shared this with me."

We had the party for the girls and they had Walls ice cream. I shared with them my story of my conversion, encouraging them to give their heart to the Lord. Nothing in God's economy is ever wasted. Plant the seed in faith and it will yield fruit.

Three years later I was in the garden. I heard someone calling, "She is here." I looked back and saw this same lady but did not recognise her. She introduced herself to me, saying, "Do you remember? I was your first Bed and Breakfast visitor. We were passing through Matlock and thought of calling to enquire how you are getting along with the Bed and Breakfast."

I said, "I have never looked back."

Another lady from South Africa had a brother living in Matlock. She had written to her brother asking him to find a place for her to stay, a Bed and Breakfast with a bath. Her brother sent her over to our address. She came and stayed a week. I took breakfast to her room. She loved it, had her daily bath and on the whole must have been well pleased. She wrote a recommendation note and asked the Red Lion pub keeper to post it on the notice board. A copy of it was sent to us. When I read it, I said to my husband, "John, this is an answer to our prayers!"

There was a time when I had students from the Teachers' Training College in Matlock. Since it closed down I have had French, Spanish and Chinese student lodgers from time to time.

I gave birth to Timothy Emmanuel 17 months later. I enjoyed every moment of motherhood. As the children grew they somehow looked alike because I used to dress them like triplets. People used to ask if they were triplets. The children, Daniel and Samuel, started junior school; a year later, Timothy joined them. Motherhood was my preferred hobby! I desired to have another child, hoping for a girl, but God knew best. On 6th March 1971 we were blessed with another son, Paul Mark Vahan. At the time of writing this I would like to mention about their achievements. Daniel became an aerospace communications engineer, working at Manchester Airport. Samuel is a consultant at London Chelsea and Westminster Hospital, Tropical Medicine Department. Timothy is working in Hull as a GP. Paul has become a pastor in Boston, Massachusetts. It is amazing how time flies.

You may not agree with what I am about to share with you. We read, "I will greatly increase your pains in childbearing" (Genesis 3:16). But we read in Colossians 2:14, "Having cancelled the written code, with its regulations, that was against us and that stood opposed to us; he took it away, nailing it to the cross." With each labour contraction I was praising the Lord. The Holy Spirit was reminding me of Scriptures to declare over this new life about to be born. I truly enjoyed going through the labour 'pains'. When I praised and kept speaking blessings for the baby, I seemed to have less pain. Better than any analgesic!

Encounter with the Lord

The Assemblies of God church in Matlock was our place of worship. We attended regularly. Each Sunday there was excitement to get to church on time. John was punctual to play the piano.

The gifts of the Holy Spirit were in evidence. The congregation came prepared to share the lessons and blessings they had gleaned through the week. Through the quiet times spent before the presence of the Lord there was spiritual soul searching and great expectation amongst the people who were present. Someone likened it to a petrol station, those who came were filled with spiritual manna, and they never went away empty.

There was Holy Communion participation each Lord's day. Whenever I missed going, due to family illness, I was anxious that I might have missed something.

Encounter 1

A week of Evangelism was held in mid-March, 1969, at the AoG church.

A young couple, who were newly qualified from theological college and had a baby daughter, ran the meetings. You see we lived in the valley, and the church was situated high up on the mountain behind our house, high up, almost at the top of a very steep hill. By this time we had been attending the AoG church for four years. I used to do most of my praying as I walked up. (This reminds me how, after pushing the large heavy twin pram half way up the 'mountain', my legs would shake and my heart would race. I had to stop using the pram and use a light pushchair instead.)

The spirit within me kept acknowledging that they had something I didn't have. I longed to know more about the things of God, Jesus and the gifts of the Holy Spirit. This language was totally new to me, as I was coming from another nation and culture.

One thing was clear. I was thirsty to have or receive what they had. One Thursday in this gathering, I no longer could hold back my deep longing. I meant business with the Lord. Determined not to be affected by any obstruction, hindrance or hysterical behaviour!

I put my hands in my coat packet, making sure I was not going to show any physical emotion! I walked to the front without being called. The Minister asked, "Why did you come?"

I said, "I want to receive the Baptism in the Holy Spirit." The Pastor told me to go to the back room. As I pushed open the door, at that very moment, I had an encounter with the Lord Jesus. I felt His powerful presence. He took hold of my two hands (which were in my coat pockets), started squeezing, gently but firmly and confronting me with questions. "Would you forgive your friend who hurt you? Would you obey and submit to my ordinances?" As He questioned my integrity, I was repenting, crying, totally yielding, "Yes, yes, Lord, anything you want. I give you my all." I was rubbing my thumb on His thumb to feel if it was real! I clung to Him and would not let Him leave me!

A few hours must have slipped past. I heard someone say, "We have to go now, it's late." I did not want to leave His presence. It was in the early hours of the morning. Someone brought me home. I went to bed, praising, thanking and worshipping the Lord. The following three days I could still feel His hands gripping mine, even when I was washing the dishes.

I would like you to picture me with four boys all under ten years of age, getting them ready for Sunday worship. We nearly always got to the church at the last minute. One Sunday we were a few minutes late, so we waited behind the closed door, waiting to hear the 'Amen'. But this time, as we opened the door, I could hear the pastor reading the words that Jesus told His disciples, "Rejoice that your names are written in heaven" (Luke 10:20). It was worth the struggle to get up there just to hear those comforting words.

While Paul was still a toddler, I found work as a kitchen assistant in Claremont Nursing Home. I took driving lessons, but failed three times. I desperately needed someone to take me on the road for driving practice. Mrs Joan took me in my car to Manchester to visit her mother, so that I could get practice. Later, my friend Dorothy took me to Tansley. We practised emerging into the road, doing three-point turns, controlling the car on a gradient without rolling back etc. Thanks to Dorothy's help, I passed the fourth time. She even came from Wirksworth to support me on the day of the test.

Twins vanish in town centre

On Thursday 15th April, 1972, in the Easter holidays, I was happy to take my four sons to Derby for a shopping treat. Paul, the youngest, was in the pushchair. We went to Derby by car and parked near the Derby Royal Infirmary. I had promised to give the children a family outing, providing they behaved well at home and at school. This was to be a treat for them.

I took them to Lego Land toyshop to choose a toy for themselves and buy some other necessities. The children had an exciting time at Lego Land and played with some other toys. We came out, found a place to eat our sandwiches, took our time wandering around the Eagle Centre and then walked towards the car park.

Suddenly I noticed the twins, Daniel and Samuel, were missing. They were not in front of me! I noticed this outside a wedding gown shop at the corner of the Eagle Centre. I looked right and left but could not see them anywhere near. I shall never forget the horror of seeing the sky over me turn to black. I felt as if a heavy blanket had been thrown over me, paralysing my senses with fear.

There was no time to waste. I started telling passers-by that my twin sons were missing. I looked for a policeman and saw one near Woolworths. He was reassuring, took the details of the twins and passed them to the local Derby radio to be broadcast. I rang my husband and told him the predicament I was in. I asked him to come and take charge of the remaining sons, Timothy and Paul, while I stayed in Derby until the twins had been found. I was not going home without them.

We both searched the area as best as we could but with no result. John took Timothy and Paul home on the train while I stayed behind and went to the police station to wait for news of the boys being found. It was getting darker. I left the police station and tried to look for them. After a few minutes walking I saw the twins walking hand in hand towards the police station. I find it very difficult to explain the joy and the relief I felt at that moment of seeing them. We walked to the police station to give them the good news that the children had made their own way to the police station.

They were just as happy as I had been. What had happened? At the corner of the wedding gown shop the twins had walked down the left side of the shop, hoping mother would follow them, but I had been expecting the boys would follow me on the right side of the shop.

Exhibition bomb blast

John, my husband, was employed by British Rail. He was enthusiastic about rail travel and his children were entitled to travel free. We made good use of this advantage and often took the children to London Zoo, Madam Tussaud's Waxwork Museum, art galleries, the Tower of London, Tower Bridge etc.

One weekend we took them to the Ideal Homes Exhibition (it was mostly my desire to see the exhibition). At the front of the great exhibition hall there was a model aeroplane. Our children played there, spending time with other boys; they played with this contraption for hours. Towards lunchtime the boys began to lose interest so we left the exhibition and made our way to the Thames to see HMS Victory.

While we were at the Thames river bank we could hear the loudspeakers announcing an explosion at the Ideal Homes Exhibition, which we had only just left a short time before. The bomb had apparently been left in a rubbish bin where the children were playing, quite unaware of the impending danger.

On our arrival home we turned on the wireless to hear the evening news. It was broadcasting the same news about the bomb explosion at the Ideal Homes Exhibition.

It made us think how God in His mercy had once again protected our family. We had very much to thank the Lord for His guidance. When we noticed that the children had lost interest in playing with that model aeroplane we had been right to leave. Had we stayed there for another half-an-hour, who could tell what it would have been like.

Ruby gem, lost and found

Most mothers have a drawer full of collections of small items, some valuable, some not so. They are kept for practical reasons. I had one such drawer in which I remember having a ring with a ruby, which fitted loosely in the setting. The ring needed to be taken to a goldsmith to have the ruby fixed more securely into the gold setting. It had been left in the drawer, waiting for the ruby to be fixed.

Before we altered our small kitchen we used to have a blue nylon floor mat. Whenever I spring-cleaned the kitchen,

I used to scrub this nylon floor mat with hot soapy water and put it on the stone wall to let it drip dry.

One day the weather changed and a strong wind blew the floor mat over to the other side of the wall, onto the footpath that runs beside our garden. I went round to the other side of the wall to pick up the mat and spotted a red sparkling glass-like bead in the shrubbery. I looked carefully, picked up this red object from the grass and, to my amazement, recognised the red ruby from my gold ring. This was nothing short of a miracle. I took it in and tried it on my ring. The ruby fitted my ring, it was mine. To make sure that it was indeed mine, I tipped out the contents of the drawer and looked to see if my ruby was still there. No, it was not.

Now the big question was: how could this precious gem have got behind the stone wall? That evening I asked all four boys: "I would like you all to speak the truth. There will be no punishment. Please tell me, who threw the ruby over the wall?"

No one admitted to having thrown the gem over the wall. Even now, I still do not know how the ruby got thrown over the wall. It remains a mystery. I find it most amazing that God knew where it was, took me behind the fence to find it and that I picked it up. In the 18 months since I had last seen it in the drawer I had not known that it was missing. Thank you Lord.

Children do have their own angels

One weekend during the school term, I took my four sons to Derby to buy school uniforms and other clothing. We were at Marks and Spencer's, having bought a few garments. Coming out of the shop there were a few steps going down, leading to very heavy glass swing-doors. Timothy had put his fingers inside the narrow opening of one of the glass swing-doors. I did not know and had not seen him put his hand in that narrow space which allows the door to open and close on its hinges.

At that very second the angel of Timothy spoke to me: "Turn round and pull the boy's hand from the door hinge area." There is no shadow of doubt in my mind that it was the child's protecting angel.

Had the angel not prompted me at that precise moment, Timothy could have lost four of his fingers. How can I not give Him praise? God is not too late in performing His acts of deliverance. His ways are past finding out.

God is watching our circumstances

In my day-to-day living there was a time of monetary shortage. I had to write a letter to someone who was waiting to hear from me. I wrote the letter. In my purse there were just enough coins to buy a postage stamp and send the letter. I had no more money left to buy food for my family.

On my return from the post office I noticed a piece of paper blown by the wind on the road. I went and had a closer look to see what it was. To my astonishment, it was a one pound note. I picked it up off the ground, took it to the lorry driver by the cash and carry shop, which was just behind the police station, and asked him if the money was his. He replied, "No duck," so I looked around to see if there were others who may have lost the pound note. As I was trying to find an owner, I heard the Holy Spirit saying, "Don't look for an owner, it is yours." I stood still for a moment trying to find out who had spoken to me. Then I realised it was the still small voice of God. That one pound gliding on the street was God's provision for my family for the week. "Don't despise the day of small things."

God Himself was by my side

It is about 16 years since I have walked through the valley of the shadow of death. I remember the day when I was dusting the staircase. The still small voice was saying, "No one shall wrench you out of my hand." God is indeed a very present help in time of trouble. I was strengthened by this command. (Praise due to Him.)

Daniel came from Glasgow airport to go to Birmingham to collect a timeshare prize. I had to follow his instructions and take him to this place. After we had found the place we were admitted into a big hall and had to wait our turn for whatever they had to offer Daniel. I had been reluctant to go with Daniel but it was not time wasted. Everyone who went there was allocated to someone who would care for them. The one who was allocated to Daniel was a very curious man. Only a week before he had interviewed a man who was out of prison and had come to this place with a large Bible under his arm, trying to win people into the kingdom of God. It was pretty obvious that this interviewer had been interested in what that man had said to him.

When he met us he told us about his encounter with the freed prisoner. Somehow he started to quiz me about what he had heard from the prisoner. It was most amazing how, at that given moment, the Holy Spirit was reminding me of the Scriptures appropriate for the questions I was being asked.

Daniel, my son, was getting a little annoyed with his mother, but God had another strategy. Firstly, it was a unique opportunity for Daniel to hear and know his mother's testimony. Secondly, I had thought that God had finished with me – that I was no more use. After I came home I realised it was not so. I had been strengthened in the inner man while the interviewer had been learning about Jesus.

God can be trusted, even when we are being tested (Genesis 22:1-19).

One of Abraham's famous words to his son Isaac was, "God Himself will provide." This trustworthy word still holds.

Here is an incident of a spiritual landmark in my home life which I would like to share with you. In the 1970s there was an article in the local newspaper asking local families if they could provide holiday accommodation for French students. We thought it would be a good thing to do for our four growing sons, so we went through all the necessary documentation to have one teenage boy from France for a week's holiday with our sons.

The day of his arrival was fixed; we had to meet him at a certain point in town and bring him home. However, the coach was delayed by a few hours, so it was decided that the children were to be taken to individual home addresses by the leaders of the group.

Everything was ready to welcome our young French guest. Incidentally, the children's arrival date coincided with the Monday on which we were having the monthly 'Ladies' Fellowship' at our home the same evening. Our sons were put to bed a little earlier and they were all fast asleep by the time the leaders arrived at our doorstep, handing over our French student boy. He was warmly welcomed, befriended, fed, washed and refreshed. We explained that the boys were in bed and were asleep, and would be up tomorrow morning to play with him. After this he was introduced to his own bedroom. Having made him comfortable, we wished him goodnight and came down.

Evidently the boy found it strange in a new environment, got anxious and fearful, thinking in his mind that he had been brought into another home where there were no children. This anxiety must have prompted him to telephone his dad in France, telling him his fear of being placed in the wrong home.

Early next morning we received numerous telephone calls from the authorities and from his father demanding the child's transfer. His father assumed that his child had been placed into the wrong address, but this was unfounded. The organisers were put under such pressure by the father that they had no alternative but to remove the child, just to satisfy him. There was no way of persuading either party. You could imagine how it felt: within a few minutes they were about to go with the teenager. In these crucial, decisive moments my Lord was whispering to me, "The Lord himself will provide."

I was glad to let them go without any animosity. I quickly went into the garden, picked the one rose that grows each year on Grandad's rose bush, and pinned it on to the lapel of the organiser's coat. As soon as they were on their way I had to hurry into the house as I heard the phone. It was an enquiry: could I accommodate five adults for a few days? You can guess the answer ... "Yes" ... The Lord has proved to be my provider.

I do hope this small true story will be of encouragement to my readers.

Meeting with Mr Zananeery

For the past few years Mr Zananeery had come to Cliff College to represent the Jordanian Christian Community Church. I had heard about this gentleman a year before and wished to meet him, but at the time this desire did not materialise.

During this period, early in the '70s, the political situation in Beirut, Lebanon was at its worst. I received indirect news from people who came away from the Beirut chaos. My niece had written a short note that was passed on to me. An SOS – "We are unable to sleep, go out or eat for fear of being targeted or kidnapped. We need help." The TV news was just as bad and sad to hear or watch. I heard the newsreader say, "Beirut is on fire!"

All four of my sons were at school; I tried to write a letter to my dear ones in Beirut. Nine months had passed since I had heard from them. The telephones were out of action. I sat trying to reach them with a message of love, care and comforting thoughts. No matter how much I tried, I could not find any sentence with which I could satisfy my desire to help or console them. In desperation, I squashed the notepaper, lay my head in my arms and cried aloud, calling for God's help, "Make a way in the wilderness!"

We had recently had a telephone installed in our house. If I remember rightly, my first telephone call was from Pat Stanbrook, asking if I was doing anything. "No, why?" She suggested taking the children to Bakewell Park, to 'Sunshine Corner' (an open-air Sunday school) led by Michael Fentom the clown.

We agreed to go and soon all eight children and the two of us were driving to Bakewell in my car.

When we got there, Mrs Beryl Briddon came and told me about Mr Zananeery. She said, "You would love to meet this man." I sat in the shadow of a tree waiting for him. He had gone to buy some sweets for his children, a boy of eight and a girl of six; his wife was left at home as she was expecting their third child. We sat in the shadow of this cedar tree while the Sunshine Corner leaders were entertaining the children.

After we had been introduced to one another, I told Mr Zananeery how much I had desired to meet him, telling him how distressed I had been that morning because I could not see how I could get in touch with my family in Beirut. I wished to send a sum of money and asked if he could help in any way.

"Yes," he said, "I know of a churchwarden who lives in Beirut. He is a very trustworthy man. We have helped needy families in Beirut during the three years of war. He will go to your sister's address and give the sum of money – as much as you want. I will write a letter to you asking you to send me the cheque. You don't need to give me any money now." Here it is once again – the Lord answered a cry of help, making a way in the wilderness.

It was Thursday, the day of prayers in our church. I asked Mr Zananeery if he would like to come for supper with his children and then to a prayer meeting. He was pleased to accept, so our children and his children played and had a wonderful time. After supper the children watched TV. I took him to our church. He passed on greetings from his community church. He said that he was a Palestinian, converted to Christianity, and had a home church in his house. This was at a time when Christians and Palestinians were fighting in Beirut. What a wonderful God we serve! "His ways are indeed past finding out." Months later I heard from him and sent him my cheque. My people safely received the sum.

Visit to Valance cancelled

I have a cousin living in Valance, France, who has five children. We were in close communication with them; they kept asking us to visit them and we also wanted to see them. We fixed a date for this visit and decided to go as a family for a week.

I started to prepare. Each time I went shopping to get gifts for my cousin's children, my mind was saying, "Your family in Beirut has more need of all these things than the cousins in France."

There had been a war in Lebanon for the past three years. Since 1975 Beirut had been in turmoil with sad news of war.

This had escalated into full-blown civil war: Jews from the south border of Lebanon were defending their territory, Syrian occupation of the land of Lebanon, policing the Palestinians, Israeli conflict, bombs dropping on the towns killing innocent people.

I heard on the TV news that Beirut was on fire. I lost sleep with worry because my uncle and family lived in the centre of the city, at the top of a skyscraper building which was used as the Italian Bank. Uncle had worked there for over 50 years as a guard in the lift. They had had a son after 20 years of marriage. On the roof of this famous Bank of Italy my uncle's wife kept a cafeteria for the office staff.

On one of those days two gentlemen came to see me for different reasons. I knew them from the church. Bill had come to give me books that he had promised and, while he was at the door, Tony Wilson came to ask if he could leave his motorbike in our backyard, so that people could come and have a look at it and test drive it before buying it. Tony had put an advert in the newspaper to sell his bike and, as our house was in the town centre, it was an easy place for potential purchasers to see the motorbike.

I took this opportunity to ask them in, and we prayed an agreed prayer for my people who were going through hard times of fear and danger. The result of this prayer was wonderful, as they were plucked out of the fire.

The Lord revealed to me a verse from Jeremiah 36:26b, "But the LORD had hidden them." This short but vital verse literally jumped out of the pages of the Bible. We later learned that my sister's house had been hit by a rocket. The settee had caught fire and had been flung off the balcony while they were all hiding by the staircase. Auntie Alice said, "Something told me to take everyone and go down to hide. The rocket came through the kitchen wall and out it went. No one was injured, praise the Lord."

Despite the fact that we had planned to visit my cousin in Valance, there was an unexplained reluctance within my spirit. I found it unreasonable to go on holiday while my dear ones living in Beirut were going through a horrendous civil war. I was very concerned about their well-being. One night I woke up with an irresistible impulse to intercede for the people of Beirut, Lebanon.

I had much to tell Jesus. While everyone was asleep, I got up in the early hours of the morning, went into the next room and poured out my heart to my friend, Jesus. Philippians 4:6 says, "Do not be anxious about anything but in everything by prayer and petition, with thanksgiving, present your request to God, and the peace of God, which passes all understanding, shall keep your heart and mind through Christ Jesus."

The Bible encourages us to ask in faith. Nothing is impossible with the Lord. He does make a way in the wilderness. He grants us the luxury of waiting. I was in this waiting period, doing household chores, I had read Psalm 37:4; it said, "Delight yourself in the LORD and He will give you the desires of your heart." I thought, "What is there to delight myself about?" At first I could not find anything to delight in, but then I began to hum some choruses. It is amazing how praising can change our turmoils into peace.

I went to the letterbox. To my amazement there was a letter from my sister in Beirut, the first in 18 months. It read, "Our only uncle, Hovhanes, his wife and their only son, Garo, have been missing for many months, perhaps over a year. No one knows where he or she can be found."

My brother, Hagop, had searched for them amongst the relatives in Kesab village, on the Syrian borders and through the length and breadth of Beirut, but without success. Hagop had even looked among the corpses floating on the Mediterranean seashore. The TV news estimated that the number of souls missing was 26,000.

My uncle had married in the Catholic Church sometime during the Second World War, because they could get married there without having to pay a fee. They never attended church. They lived and worked at the Italian Bank in the centre of Beirut.

In her letter my sister said that the last time they had seen Uncle Hovhanes was when he had paid them a visit in the midst of the civil war. My brothers had told him to bring his wife and son to the east of Lebanon to stay with them.

He had told them, "Don't worry, we'll be all right. The Syrian soldiers are bringing bread when we ask them, and we have lots of canned food. We are safe." So he had refused to accept help and had gone back to his wife and son. This was the last communication with my brothers. There had been no trace of my uncle and his family for 18 months since then.

I understood from my sister's letter that Hagop, after searching for nine months and failing to trace the whereabouts of their bodies, had consulted a solicitor. The solicitor had told him that he would have to hold a funeral in order to obtain documentation showing that he, his brother and two sisters were the next of kin. Then attempts could be made to retrieve the money uncle may have saved within the bank! He had to pay to get his rights met. In short, he was eventually granted a document by the authorities to become the recipient of uncle's money.

An official letter was enclosed in my sister's letter, all written in Arabic and signed and stamped. A quarter of the estate was to be claimed by me. To conclude, my sister had written saying that I could either claim this sum or come and collect it from the bank, taking this document with me as evidence. Well, what can I say? This was nothing short of an answer to prayers. There were no two ways about it, my mental unease had been solved.

This provided me with a fair reason for writing to my cousin in Valance and asking him to understand why we had to cancel our trip to Valance and, God willing, we would see them the next year.

Much later we discovered the horrible truth, that the whole family had been murdered and their bodies thrown from the skyscraper roof where they had lived.

8
Grandfather's salvation and his home call

In 1972, Daniel, our eldest son, twin brother to Samuel, became ill with an asthmatic attack in his second year at school. The doctor was called and Daniel was transferred to Derby Children's Hospital. He was examined by a paediatrics doctor and was put into an oxygen tent. Doctor Charles was informed. He and his wife Lucien (they were the godparents) came to assess the situation.

The paediatrician told me, "Daniel will be all right to go home the day after tomorrow." With that hope I was able to leave him after he was sleeping peacefully in the oxygen tent. Doctor Charles drove me home to Matlock. Paul was about nine months old. My neighbour Mrs Heweth had been asked to look after Paul, fetch Samuel and Timothy from school and look after him until I returned. Daniel responded to the treatment and was brought home. I am glad to mention that he has never had any such breathing difficulty since.

I had a distinct dream that night.

The dream

I was fast asleep in my dream. Someone apparently tried to wake me up but could not. Then someone put his hand on my shoulder and shook me firmly to rouse me from my deep sleep (I believe this must have been an angel). I began to wake up very reluctantly, I could hear him say, "You have already missed one episode. You must not miss this one. You must wake up and take notice of what you have been shown." I eventually woke up, hardly able to shake myself from my slumber. I struggled to see what the urgency was.

I saw large heavy curtains split open to reveal a theatre stage. The only thing on the platform was a huge empty green bottle, large round-based with a narrow neck.

I looked at this and thought to myself, "Was it worth waking me up for this scene?" I opened my eyes to have a closer look at this large empty bottle. As I kept looking, the neck of the bottle began to stretch up and up towards heaven. It took the shape of a hungry and thirsty bird's beak. It kept stretching with such gusto, I became aware that it was becoming alive. At that precise moment I heard a thundering loud voice from heaven; hands holding a large heavy pitcher filled with water started pouring the water into this empty vessel, filling it to overflowing. The voice was so powerful, I believe it was God's voice declaring His word from Isaiah 44:3, "I will pour water on the thirsty land, and streams on the dry ground." I saw the water being poured and overflowing, covering the dry ground. To my amazement, scores of angels surrounded the overflowing bottle. I joined in this group of angels and rejoiced with them. Then I woke up out of my sleep, woke my husband and told him the vision. (I related this dream to my dad's salvation.)

In the course of time I received a letter from Naomi, my sister, informing me about my dad's illness, that he was in hospital with a high fever, his lungs full of purulence. Would we pray for his soul!

Miss Helen Cawood, an art teacher and my long-standing prayer partner, was visiting us. We both knelt down at the sofa in the back living room and prayed for my dad to acknowledge Jesus as his personal Saviour.

Let me remind you that earlier in my story I had mentioned my puny attempt to convert Dad and that it had ended in my being abused. Since then I had given him over to God's capable hands.

My dad was a heavy smoker. I remember him advising my brothers not to take up smoking. He had told them that he regretted not being able to stop. The whole family suffered because of his smoking.

A week later another short letter from my sister said, "Dad

has discharged himself from the hospital." He was brought home and was being cared for by my mother. His general practitioner, Dr Roport Chorbajian, was a Christian too, and he must have had considerable influence upon Dad's conversion. Dad was swamped with prayers. Four days before he died he admitted that he was a sinner, confessed Jesus as his Saviour and asked my mother to sing hymns for him. According to my mother's testimony, Dad's conversion was very sincere and genuine. He had thrown his arms into the air calling for God to have mercy on him, to accept him as he was. He was assured of his salvation.

When I read the letter, I too believed he had full salvation because of the vision that God had shown me in my dream – the empty vessel being filled with His water of life, the empty bottle becoming alive by stretching towards heaven. There shall be rejoicing over one sinner who repents, and it was so in my vision – angels dancing around this bottle after it had been filled to overflowing.

It was Thursday, our church prayer and Bible study night. I went to church and when the minister asked if there were any special needs to bring for prayer I jumped to my feet, eager to give the good news of Dad's conversion and his home call. I was not ashamed to tell friends at church that I love my dad more now than I had when he was alive. I shall see him in heaven; he will welcome me with my three baby sisters.

My conclusion is: the very habit he was entangled with, his smoking, was the means of his conversion. Alleluia!

Later that year my pastor from Beirut came to London with his wife on their way to California. We went down to London as a family to see them. They sat me between them, both put their arms on my shoulders and told me how my dad had totally surrendered his life to Jesus Christ a few days before he passed away. I told them how the Lord had shown me the vision of the empty bottle being filled with his spirit, the water of life.

So, my dear reader, I encourage you to keep on believing and praying. What is impossible with man is possible with God.

9

First family visit to Beirut, 1977

Following the news of the official letter enclosed in my sister's letter, I did not hesitate about deciding to take my husband and four sons, all under twelve years of age, to Beirut. I wrote home and told them of my intention to visit them within six weeks. The first thing we did was to pray for guidance. Then we started planning.

I had an old car. Its MOT was about to expire in six weeks. I thought of having it checked by a mechanic, to make sure it was sound enough to take the family to the airport and back. Meanwhile, John would enquire how much it would cost to insure the whole family for three weeks. John had to extend his annual holiday by one more week, making it three in total.

We also wrote to cousin John Polatian, who lived in London, to ask if he could help us through the London traffic to Heathrow Airport and then store the car in his yard. He and his wife agreed and we were very thankful for their help and hospitality.

There is another point that I want to make clear. I normally do not believe in paying insurance, but simply trust in God's promises. But this time the circumstances were entirely different, since we were taking four young children to a country torn with strife and civil war. The children were born in Britain and I would not have liked any harm to come to them. A day after we prayed, John was to enquire at some travel agents in Derby about the cost of insuring the whole of the family's flight to and from Beirut.

I was about my usual household chores, hoovering the rooms between the front sitting room and back room. I had this unusual impulse, saying, "Sit down and read Psalm 121." This impulse kept on and on for 20 minutes, when my mind suggested something out of the ordinary. I stopped and questioned, "Should I? Why should I?" I started giving reasons, saying it wasn't the time to read Psalm 121. I knew it almost by heart, as I had listened to it on tape not so long ago. Well, no excuse would stop the compelling voice. "Sit down and read Psalm 121."

I suddenly thought, "Is Jesus trying to say something to me? Speak Lord, your servant is listening." I put aside my hoovering, picked up my Bible and read Psalm 121. I read very carefully the first verse, but there was no specific word for the present situation. I read through with expectancy and when I came to the eighth verse, it read, "The LORD will watch over your coming and going both now and FOR EVERMORE." Hey! My whole family's insurance in God's promise. I jumped with joy – we had been concerned for only three weeks' insurance yet God was saying, "I will watch over you for evermore." This was a direct word of promise from my Saviour, a 'rhema word'.

I could hardly wait for John to come home. He arrived from work, stood at the kitchen door and began to pull out a strip of paper. On it he had written the three travel agents' insurance quotations. I interrupted him and told him, "The Lord has spoken through His Word. We are to depend on His promise and not to spend money for insurance. Instead, use that money for more essential needs, i.e. for purchasing tickets." Relying on His unfailing Word, I have travelled without insurance to the USA five times, Canada seven and Europe three times.

Regarding the old car, to make it roadworthy

I took the car to Tansley Ford Garage. The engineer tested the car and told me it had failed with four points. He said it was repairable but would cost £80. I tried to explain to him, that I would pay the £80 after we had returned from Beirut. What money we had would not pay for our tickets. He told me, "Mrs Allen, you cannot take the car out of the garage without paying first."

(I was not intending to keep the car after its MOT expired, but wanted to make sure it would be safe to travel to and from Heathrow.) Leaving the car behind at the garage I walked all the way home, praying as I made the half-hour's journey.

I went to the postbox to see if any bills had arrived. I found a small brown envelope addressed to me. I opened it and found a cheque for £300, sent anonymously. You can imagine my joy and I was filled with praise. I took the cheque to the bank to withdraw £80 to pay for the car repair.

The repairs to the car were supposed to be finished by 4pm. I walked back to the garage with light-hearted steps. When I got there, the manager had in his office a very rich, highly made up lady, so he made sure I would not bring my plea to him in front of this swanky lady. I waited behind the door until this lady left. It was considerate of him. I was yearning to tell him how the Lord had met my need by putting in someone's heart to send a cheque of £300. I knew of no one but God who knew our situation. I give Him the glory and the praise.

The day arrived. We were ready, I drove to the Polatians' home in London. We changed into their car and Uncle Polatian drove us to Heathrow. He knew the way as he used to travel to Europe with his business.

The whole family boarded the Lebanese airplane and within six to seven hours we were over Lebanon. The air conditioner was turned off, I was stripping off the layers of clothing from the children's backs when Samuel said, "Wouldn't it be good if we had a crash – I would be able to swim in this blue Mediterranean Sea." I said to him with confidence, "No, son, it will not happen, God had promised to take us safely to Beirut and back home. He also even promised to be with us for evermore."

It will take pages to record all our feelings and emotions. When we sat in my sister's lounge, we could not exchange words. There was an awesome silence. We just looked at each other with deep gratitude toward God.

My sister had been working for twelve months in the health clinic, giving rations to the needy. She had four weeks' holiday to cater for all of us. We enjoyed a very exciting time with our dear ones. They organised trips to historic places of interest. My desire was to have a day at the sea, so we went with four car-loads and tried to swim and get our bodies tanned.

They asked us to stay another week, but John had to start work. They all came to see us off at the airport. We arrived home safely, but a letter received later said, "What a good thing you left Beirut when you did." They had been forced to hide and run on their way back. The shooting and bombing had started again. The airport was closed down and we had been the last to leave the airport.

John's healing

A fortnight after we returned from our trip to Beirut, John began to pass urine stained with blood. We were rather alarmed and asked the GP for a urine test. This proved that our fears were justified – a high percentage of red blood cells was found in his urine. An appointment was made to have a diagnostic test under general anaesthetic. The appointment was fixed for the following Monday morning.

Incidentally, that Saturday prior to the appointment, there had been healing meetings held in Matlock Town Hall at 7.30pm. The guest speaker, who was a divine healer, an American, was a man of extraordinary character. He was humorous, over-weight and wore red trousers and a white shirt. Most of us were captured by the clean, interesting, humorous healing stories that he told us, one after the other. It really did raise the audience's faith.

I encouraged John to attend the Saturday night healing meeting, which was the last one to be held. John would have preferred not to (he is so timid), but he inwardly feared that the outcome of his urinary tract investigation (which was due in two days) might change his life in the future.

John attended the Saturday evening meeting. The message was inspiring – it was about God's all-enabling power to heal any need, however small it may be. As long as we have faith in His almighty power it is at our disposal, if we do not doubt and give Him the glory.

So when the minister gave his first call, "Who wants to be healed?" John spontaneously left his seat without any prompting. He went to the front. The preacher prayed, "You are healed (go in faith)." John came and sat back in his place.

On Monday we attended Chesterfield Royal Hospital. After he had undergone the test and recovered from the anaesthetic, we came home. We were anxious to know the result of the test and kept asking if the GP had received any news. Yes, but the print on the report was not legible, he had to send it back for a reprint. An appointment given for a check up in three months was cancelled because of heavy snow. The roads were closed. John said, "I am healed." He had accepted his healing and declared it.

In the 27 years since the incident, he has never had any problems with his water works. We believe he was healed because of his faith in God's healing power.

Family visit to Valance

Now that we had been to Beirut with the family and enjoyed every moment of it, my mind was settled from its worries concerning the effect of the war situation in Lebanon. We were ready to fulfil our promise to visit my cousin's family in Valance.

We travelled by train to London, changed trains and got one which took us to Dover harbour on the coast of England. From there we went by ferry to Calais harbour and then by train to Valance. On arrival my cousin Hagop met us. He took us to his home. We exchanged gifts. Their five and our four children got on most happily. There was no stress and everyone took part in making the stay pleasant.

When we first entered my cousin's home, we met Samuel Sevadjian, my other auntie's son, who had come from Beirut to look for a job in France. He was trying to emigrate to France to move his family from the war situation. But his plans had not materialised, so he was on his way to look elsewhere.

We enjoyed our trip to the south of France. We took the children to the Mediterranean seashore where we spent the day swimming. Another day we took them to the zoo and visited a convent with a church on top of a high mountain peak where there was a large statue of Mary in gold. We had a glorious time in an orchard. From there we went to a T-shirt factory and the children were presented with T-shirts, after which we returned home.

Each night the families had a time of worship. They had to ask forgiveness from one another if they had hurt anyone's feelings or misbehaved in any way that disturbed their conscience. I believe this was the main reason for the families' strong bond of unity, humility and obedience. We visited two evangelical churches and met with old friends who were immigrants from Beirut.

I believe this was another of God's appointments. I was eager to find out how my immediate family had fared in the past year. Since I had met them in 1977, my cousin Samuel told me that my sister's house had suffered a direct hit from a rocket. The armchair had caught fire, so they had hurled it off the balcony. I asked him, "Where were they at the time of this rocket's devastating blow?"

Samuel said, "They were hiding on the ground floor staircase." As I heard this, my spirit was saying that the Lord had told me through the Scriptures, "But the LORD had hidden them" (Jeremiah 36:26b). (God gave this rhema word, months before, when three of us had prayed).

On 15th August, 1978, as we were ready to leave, someone handed me a slip of paper which was a message from my sister, telling us that the Albarian family was arriving in England at Heathrow Airport on 18th August, on their way to Canada, and asking if we would meet them and bring them to Matlock for a week.

This was indeed exciting news. We said our goodbyes to our dear ones in Valance and boarded the train to Paris. On our arrival in Paris, we took the children to the Eiffel Tower and were just in time to catch the train back to Calais seaport. When we passed through customs, we were given the all clear. The children were so good, I praised God for my lovely sons and for our safe arrival home in Matlock. We had just enough time to unpack and prepare for my sister's family's arrival in two days time, before going to meet them at Heathrow and bring them to my home in Matlock.

We planned our days ahead. John carried on as usual with his work and the children knew what was expected of them. I had a map drawn to take myself for the first time to London on my own. I took my time making my way along the complicated busy roads. I parked the car, went to the arrival lounge, saw many passengers arriving and leaving, but no sign of my sister's family. I went to enquire whether their aeroplane, which was coming from Amsterdam, had arrived. I was told that it had arrived two hours ago, so I wondered where they were.

I was getting tired of looking for them. The staff was going off duty; the corridors were getting emptier. Then I tried once again to go and ask the receptionist. I was told that I was in the wrong terminal. I would have to walk along the underground escalator, along long corridors to get to the correct terminal. After half-an-hour of fast walking in the middle of the night I eventually arrived, walked up the steps and aimed to find them by asking at the enquiry desk. Suddenly I saw my brother-in-law at the enquiry desk and ran towards him. We were pleased to have found each other. He took me to where they were sitting waiting for me. They had been prepared to sleep on the steps, so were more than pleased to see me. We gathered all their belongings, found our way to the car park and drew out of the airport complex.

On my way back from Heathrow I lost my sense of direction and could not follow the map I had drawn. We circled for an hour, trying to find the way to the M1 so we could get back home. Those who directed us were also wrong in their instructions. I should not have asked them. Finally I was following the right route and we arrived home at 4am. They had a drink, went to bed and slept like babies. They were exhausted.

After a good rest, we had our meal and took them to Chatsworth House. During their five days with us, we showed them around. We were proud of where God had placed us in the Derbyshire Dales, to bring up our sons. One of my deepest desires was to share my blessings with my dear ones; this desire was met in full. Again this was the Lord's doing. Glory goes to him.

At the end of five days, I took them back to Heathrow. They had to reclaim their larger suitcases out of storage. The due sum was paid and they boarded the airplane full of hope for a smart new life in Canada.

(As far as I was concerned this was one less family to worry about.)

Starting to look for work

Now that the children were all at school I was considering looking for a nursing career. I prayed for a suitable opening. One day I happened to read a newspaper and my attention was caught by an advert: 'Staff nurse vacancy at Bakewell Cottage Hospital.' This appealed to me, so I decided to apply.

I had applied before we had gone on holiday to Valance. I was accepted after an interesting interview. They were aware of my family commitments, and I had told them that I couldn't start before 15th September when the children would be settled at their school.

Alistair Macpherson drove me to Bakewell. All the way I was telling him how the Lord had been leading me to the present day. He drove me back and left to go home.

As soon as I got into my house the telephone was ringing. I picked up the receiver and it was from the Cottage Hospital. This is what they said, "Mrs Allen, since you left the office, we have been thinking about your four young children and their safety whilst you are at work in Bakewell." They told me, "It's too far for you to travel to work; there is going to be another vacancy available nearer to your home in Matlock. The Matron of Whitworth Hospital has been contacted regarding your application and we have passed all your documents on to her. She will be meeting you at the Smedley's Hospital on Bank Road on Monday at 2pm. Would you accept this arrangement?" She continued, "We thought this arrangement might be the best for you. What do you think?" I was over the moon! I accepted the offer of their kind thoughts.

On Monday, I met with the Matron of the Whitworth hospital, signed the documents as part-time staff nurse to work 22 hours per week. I soon picked up the routine procedures of the hospital.

A short time after I had been working in the local hospital, I felt an obvious sense of general resentment towards me by two local auxiliary nurses who had been there for many years. They were friendly with the matron, so they could pull the strings as and when they wished. If anything went wrong it was rolled on to my name, even when I was not on duty and knew nothing about those particular complaints against me. They tried many carnal tricks to show their dislike towards me, possibly because of my accent. They would not take any request from me, no matter how discreet I was.

I was the only staff nurse when I was on duty. There were two auxiliary nurses to help me and do the things I asked them to do. I tried to work with them, but as soon as I joined them they would leave the ward and go to the other side. In short, I sensed an increasing conflict and felt rejected.

One day I could not take it any longer. I felt like walking out. This was a clear indication of pressure rising at home as well as in the hospital. That weekend I was told that I would be transferred to Smedley's Hospital, very near my home. At first I did not take this change sitting down. I felt the bottom of my life had dropped out; I felt hopeless.

When I got home I took myself to bed, determined not to cook or do anything for the children. I was indeed at the point of having a nervous breakdown. I cried non-stop and fell sleep. When I woke up, a tender Holy Spirit was whispering, "Pick up your 'daily bread' reading, the Armenian version." I obeyed: "Do not take revenge, my friends, but leave room for God's wrath, for it is written: 'It is mine to avenge; I will repay,' says the Lord" (Romans 12:19). As I opened the book (a present from a dear friend) on 15th April the title read, "Open not your mouth, vengeance is mine, I will repay says the Lord." At the time, I was feeling like kicking everything that came in my way!

I recognised the enemy's voice buffeting me; I stood on the Word of God that I had just been reading. I began to count the blessings and the advantages of working at the Smedley's Hospital, only a stone's throw away from my home.

The working hours would be more suitable, I wouldn't have to waste time in travelling, nor use the car which had failed its MOT. I'd be spending more time at home to care for the children and feed them before going to work the evening shift and, as all the boys were learning to use their bicycles, if ever they needed their mum they could call me.

On Saturday I went round to the Smedley's Hospital to introduce myself, saying "I am starting on Monday, would you show me around? And I would like to learn the names of the patients and how they are being treated etc."

> *"Give thanks in all circumstances, for this is God's will for you in Christ Jesus."*
>
> (1 Thessalonians 5:18)

I can truly say God's hands plucked me out of an impossible situation. It was time for me to give thanks, for this had been the will of God concerning me. I was happy to work at the Smedley's Hospital.

After 18 months we were informed that the NHS would be closing down the Smedley's Hospital. I had inward peace, hoping this would open up a district job for me, but it was not to be. The authorities were asking for voluntary retirement for those who had been working over and above their retirement age.

I was asked to have an interview with the administrator. She asked me what I would prefer. I said, "I would not mind going into the district," so she asked whether I would mind going back to the Whitworth. I replied, "Not at all, I will go to wherever you appoint me."

By this time the children were used to a normal school life and were quite independent; they walked to and from school with their friends. There was always a meal ready for them on their return from school.

I went back to the Whitworth and started where I had left off. Within two weeks those two auxiliary nurses found work elsewhere and left. An older lady who had five children replaced them. She was a heavy smoker and a real bully! She wasted time, in and out of the toilet, smoking... Sadly, she died after being in and out of hospital. I attended the funeral. It was sad to see her five children lose their mother.

At times like this I had Scripture verses in my pocket. I used to recite and remind myself of God's faithful word, e.g. "Humble yourself, therefore, under God's mighty hand, that He may lift you up in due time" (1 Peter 5:6), and, "After you have suffered a little while, will Himself restore you and make you strong, firm and steadfast" (1 Peter 5:10).

Our sons were in their teens, taking an interest in sports, running in races and coming home in muddy shoes and clothing. They had to be washed, dried and re-used every weekend. One day I had all morning to wash, dry and iron the family's sheets, make the beds and the meals before going on duty by 1.45pm. I had a twin washing machine to load and unload. As I stood doing this job, my mind and heart were racing. I was tired physically, endeavouring to finish the household chores and be on time to work at 1.45pm. In a fleeting moment a thought passed through my mind, "I have never been ill, nor had a headache." I wished I did. This was a kind of cry to God, because I was truly tired working against the clock! I was also hoovering the rooms at the same time.

Suddenly something happened: I felt pain in my chest and my chest began to get a feeling of tightening. I tried to carry on hoovering, but within a few moments I could not breathe because of the tightening of my chest wall. It was as though someone was winding a rope around my chest wall. I had to sit down on the steps. A few minutes later I thought, "It will be too late to ring and tell the staff nurse in charge that I am not coming." Instead I said, "I'll be late by ten minutes, I have had chest pains."

I went to the garden to raise the alarm, let the neighbours know. Jane saw me and when I called her to come over and help to hang the linen to dry, she came to my aid.

I drove myself to Whitworth Hospital. Sister Bond sat me down and called my GP. My blood pressure was alarming, so they called an ambulance and transferred me to Walton Hospital for further tests and X-rays. I stayed in for two nights until the tests proved negative. I was discharged and sister asked the GP to give me a sick-note for three months. This I truly deserved.

During this time I received a telephone call from London. Miss Betts, a former matron in Beirut, had become a representative of Save the Children Association. She had been in Cambodia to rescue children from the war. I had seen her on TV and had written to her to tell her how much I appreciated her work.

This is what she rang me for: "I am going to buy you a ticket. You are to sit with me in the airplane; we are going to help the children in Beirut; you know the language and with your nursing capacity you could be a great asset to us in the Save the Children organisation." She asked if I would go to London to meet with them.

I went and found the headquarters of the Save the Children organisation. By the time I got there everything had changed. I was told the trip to Beirut had been cancelled because too many charities were going, taking with them more ammunition. They were very upset by this accusation. So I came home quite disappointed.

However, my sick period was over, so I returned to work. This time quite a lot of changes had taken place within the whole of the system. I had to be retrained and it was my turn to gain experience in casualty.

One Saturday we went to Belper shopping centre, to the Co-op. I heard through the loudspeaker that Beirut Airport was reopened after the massacre of the Palestinian Shatila Camp in 1982. This triggered my dashed hopes wide open to try and go and bring my mother over. She was destitute because her house had been pulled down to make wider roads.

In my next annual holiday I went back to Beirut (this was my third visit) and attempted to bring my mother with me. But though I had advised my brothers to get her visa, they had hardly been able to move about in the town to try and find the British Embassy, which was constantly changing office for reasons of security.

The day I arrived in Beirut, my brother Hagop met me and took me to my younger brother Bedros' home, where all the remaining relatives were gathered for a meal and thanksgiving.

Our custom is that the eldest son of the family bares the responsibility of caring for their old parents. Therefore Hagop told me, in front of the family, "Dear sister, we will take care of Mother. It will be difficult for Mother to leave us behind and she will have difficulty communicating with your family, as she does not speak English." So this matter was settled, I spent my time in her flat, cleaning, mending, and repairing broken windows. There was no point in replacing the window-panes, as they would shatter each time rockets hit the area. My mother was a kind-hearted woman; she was given clothing which she had not worn but had given away to more needy people. My sister-in-law was not very happy. However, I left them in God's mercy and returned to Matlock.

By 1985 the stressful situation at work in the hospital was becoming too much. I was advised to see my GP and he gave me a sick-note for six weeks. I had been invited to Canada by my nephew to his ordination. I said, "How can I take part? I am off sick." But the GP was kind enough to give me thera-peutic convalescent leave to go to Canada. Change is as good as medicine. Receiving the GP's advice to take a short thera-peutic break as well as an invitation to Daniel's (my nephew's) ordination was not a coincidence; but it was God's incident at a time when I was thinking that such an opportunity would not be possible in the state I was in (mentally, physically and emotionally drained). With God all things are possible. I believe God was in control of opening this new door for me to accept the invitation to go for the ordination. This matter was discussed with the family and they all agreed, so preparations were undertaken. I even received an anonymous gift of money to help me to go.

I received a phone call from Auntie Alice Albarian, saying, "he aeroplane you are flying on to Montreal Dorval Airport will be continuing its flight to Toronto half-an-hour later, after it has touched down at Montreal Dorval Airport. So please, stay on the airplane to come to Toronto, as we too are travelling to Toronto on the same day. We shall meet you at Toronto Airport at precisely the same time as your airplane touches down." This was just amazing news, and just in time, otherwise I would have been stranded in Dorval Airport, all on my own, not knowing what to do. In those days we did not have the luxury and convenience of cell phones.

The relatives and guests were all housed in the homes of church members. I was accommodated in Daniel's brother-in-law's house. We watched a video of Susan and Daniel's first baby, Priscilla, being born.

The following day the ordination took place in the First Armenian Evangelical Church of Toronto and was followed by a reception. I was glad to have made the effort to be there; feeling thirsty and jet-lagged, I drank coffee by the litre.

Later that evening, we went to Susan's mother's house, as it was their custom to thank the Lord after such an event. We gathered for a time of prayer and thanksgiving. At the end of it my sister suddenly remembered to look for the car keys in order to travel back to Montreal the following day. We looked everywhere, but they were nowhere to be found. Panic was about to set in for my sister, so Auntie Alice and I quickly entered the bedroom, got on our knees and prayed for divine intervention!

It was assumed that Daniel's brother, Sam, and sister, Liza, had the car keys in one of their pockets and had forgotten to leave them behind for their brother, Joel, to drive us back to Montreal.

Sam and Liza had had to return to Montreal the same night, as they had work to attend to. Due to my sister's quick thinking she phoned her son, Joel, who was staying with his friends that night. When he heard about the missing keys, Joel and his friends got into their car and made their way straight to the next train station. Hoping to gain time by catching the train before it left the station, all four young men dashed through the barriers to get to the train bound for Montreal. They all jumped into different carriages looking for Sam and Liza.

Sam and Liza had just settled down to sleep during their

long night's journey to Montreal and were oblivious to the panic they were causing. Within a moment or two, they were found by one of the young men who asked them to hand over the car keys in their pocket. As soon as the keys had been handed over they shouted to each other, "Found!" and jumped out of the train just in time. The station security guards were all in utter confusion as to what was taking place. This is a rather humorous incident, yet I reckon there was prayer behind it all.

Another remarkable thing also happened on this return journey. Joel, the eldest of three brothers, used to deal in cars. The car he had used to come to Toronto was greatly worrying him. He thought it had a broken shaft and he was planning to leave it behind. Alice and I prayed and asked God to perform a miracle, that Joel may believe that God does answer prayers.

The following day Joel changed his mind and decided not to leave the car in Toronto but drive it back home. Alice and I took turns to sit in Joel's car and keep praying for an uneventful journey home. Every now and again we heard Joel speaking to himself, "It's running all right, I can't believe this." We stopped twice en route for something to eat, such as Kentucky Fried Chicken! This gave us a chance to change seats. It was a long tiring journey and took seven to eight hours. We arrived home in the early hours of the morning. We asked Joel what he thought of the car. He simply said, "Nothing wrong. It's a miracle!"

This trip to Toronto and Montreal in 1985 was my first.

A dog called Rex

As Christmas 1978 approached, our neighbour's little dog, Phoebe, had seven puppies. The next thing we noticed was our four sons sitting in a row on the couch and in one accord asking to have one of the puppies. They said, "We don't need any Christmas gifts but just a puppy that we saw being born; we want you to buy it for us." Personally I was not very keen at first, but seeing the boys promising to look after it, it was decided to buy one for £18. I was thinking that as we were away most of the day it might be a good idea to have a dog to guard the house in our absence.

I had newly started working. It was a new subject of discussion – who was to feed the dog and take it for walks etc. The boys took it in turn to care for it but, as usual, for only a brief period of time. Soon their excitement wore off and it was left to Mum and Dad to look after it.

Our neighbour also had four children, the same age as ours. She was a single parent, and had a demanding job in the district as District Nursing Supervisor. She used to come home late in the evenings and let the dog, Phoebe, out into the night until she, Mrs Noris, was ready to go to bed, usually about midnight. She would call her dog into the house, and Phoebe used to bark for some time before settling down to sleep. Phoebe's bark used to wake our dog, Rex, because Phoebe's bed was on the other side of our kitchen wall, where Rex's bedding was. So here we used to go – every night, as soon as Phoebe was brought in, its barking would wake Rex, and we would have a long chorus of barks between Rex and his mother, Phoebe. This went on for months and years. We got so fed up and we did not know what to do. Finally we decided to place an advert and give Rex away. A lady was interested and took Rex to her home for her grandson. The following day she brought him back, the reason being that Rex was too powerful for the grandson and was jumping over the fence onto the road. We tried many adverts to find a home for Rex. This was causing a rift between husband and wife, arguing about whose turn it was to go down and stop the barking.

The situation between my husband and me was getting very tense. I said to my husband, "Either the dog goes or I must – it's playing havoc with my nerves."

At a ladies' prayer meeting in Kay's home I felt the need to ask for prayer for a solution, so that the Lord could help us somehow to resolve the tense situation at home caused by these howling dogs!

We placed another advert, 'Dog for a suitable home – free.' There were several replies. Helen and I visited all the homes to see which one was most suitable. Finally, it was decided to give the dog to a lady who showed much interest in adopting our Rex. (She wanted to raise puppies to sell.) She lived in

Wirksworth, six miles away.

At the end of the day the children came from school looking for the dog. I said, "It has gone to Wirksworth." They were very disgruntled, sad and angry with me.

"You selfish mother; why did you give away our dog? We want it back!" Now I was in a dilemma; I had not thought it would cause such a big hassle.

I prayed earnestly, "Lord, if I have done the wrong thing, I am sorry. Please let the dog come back." The next day, I took my shopping bag and went out. To my greatest surprise, our next door neighbour, Mrs Noris' house had a 'for sale' sign. I did not hesitate to go in and enquire. Mrs Noris said that her childhood boyfriend had asked her to marry him. As he had a larger home in London they were moving in a month's time. Then Mrs Lee came in the afternoon bringing nearly 20 kilos of meat from their restaurant freezer, because the meat was out of date. Now I had a fridge full of meat and no dog, so I started giving away dog meat to friends.

On the ninth day, Rex followed the school bus from Wirksworth to Matlock. When Ruth got off the school bus, she recognised Rex and brought him home saying, "I found Rex at the Matlock bus station."

I was relieved to see Rex back; he stayed with us for 18 years. I believe this was God's answer to prayer. Not only did Rex return home, but we also had a happier family, peaceful nights, ample dog food and a secure home for Rex. There was also a better future for my neighbour and her family in a bigger and better home in London with her new husband.

I resumed work after returning from my brief visit to Toronto and Montreal.

By this time our sons were already at university. Daniel was at Brunei University in Bristol studying aerospace communications engineering, Samuel was at St Andrew's University reading medicine, Timothy Emmanuel was at Dundee University reading medicine and Paul was at Broomfield College studying farm management. Paul was the top student and received four trophies at his graduation. Three of our sons graduated in the same year.

Their childhood days had been full of excitement. They attended regular Sunday services and Sunday schools and in their turn they requested water baptism, after confessing their faith in Christ Jesus.

They took part in sports activities, music lessons, air cadets, cycling, running, swimming, travelling and camping etc.

They were never spoiled with gifts or pocket money, but their essential needs were always met. There was keen competition between them. They took part in cross-country races and came back holding trophies and certificates, and Duke of Edinburgh Awards. Timothy received a first national honour for reading the Bible (with a black eye – a day before the national competition in London, Timothy was hit by a cricket ball which caught his right eye and made it swell up).

John and I visited Auntie Berthe (our Swiss friend) after she moved into a residential home. She was sat by the window of a small room, isolated from all the other residents and staff. I was disturbed to see her so unhappy and feeling lonely. I said, "If you are not happy, you might as well come and live with us. Paul will love you as his grandma." On our way back, at the bus stop, I said to John, "I think I did the wrong thing." He asked why. "I would have to give up my work before I could look after Berthe."

The day after we came home there was a phone call from the matron of the residential home. "Berthe wishes to come and be looked after by you."

I said, "But I must first give up my work."

She said, "You don't have to, you only have to help her with her bath." I could not refuse the request, so within a few days I had to go to London and bring her home to Matlock.

Her documents were passed onto me. I had great responsibility sorting out her finances. I had to get in touch with the solicitors and trustees, and her relatives had to be informed.

There was a great deal of financial, pension and banking red tape that had to be sorted. I had to handle all these matters through the solicitors; power of attorney was given to me through the solicitors etc.

However, even though she was loved and cared for to the

best of our ability she became difficult and demanded a great deal of my time. Gradually it became noticeable that she was orchestrating trouble between me and my husband. I could not believe what I was hearing – she told my husband that I had to see the social services and transfer her to a more suitable residential home in the area. After much searching and enquiry we found a Christian residential home for Berthe in Pinxton, near South Normanton.

Berthe's coming caused a lot of difficulty with my hospital duties. I had to leave work. I was going through several crises including Berthe's situation and my own health. I had an accident at work, which resulted in a breast operation. I had to go through four general anaesthetics in 18 months.

As the solicitor was sorting out Berthe's money, we went along with the advice we were given and opened a Standard Life insurance policy, but within 18 months it crashed.

My mother sent to England

Cousin Samuel Sevajian from Beirut wrote twice informing us of my mother's destitute situation. She was having difficulty in living on her own, fearing to cross the streets in case of being knocked over by the unruly fast-moving traffic. Samuel made us aware of Mother's need to be cared by her daughters, both being nurses. However, we were far away in other countries. We were aware of Mother's situation, particularly after Bedros' family had emigrated to Canada, causing further insecurity for her.

After my attempt to bring my mother to England had failed in 1982, my sister hired a solicitor in Montreal, had some documents drafted and gave them to her son, Joel, to take to Beirut and bring Grandmother out of the war situation. Joel flew to Beirut with an attempt to bring Grandmother out. Because of the civil war in Beirut, the British Consulate and Embassy could not easily be reached – security was so tight that they had to change addresses. Because he was short of time, Joel bought a ticket for Grandmother without getting a visa and sent her to me in England, saying, "Let Ovsanna sort it out, once she gets to England."

The consequence of this action caused me to suffer depression. I was already suffering stress after losing my work and the situation with Berthe, who had just left my hands.

Now we were looking forward to accommodating mother. Obviously this was the only way to rescue a 78-year-old elderly lady from the chaotic civil war in Lebanon. Our main purpose was to look after our elderly Mother's welfare. Much prayer had gone up to God for her safety. A telephone call from Joel confirmed that our prayers were taking effect. We had only just secured Berthe's welfare, so my mother's coming was just in time. I was very glad to bring her home from Heathrow Airport.

The day of her arrival was a Thursday, church prayer meeting day. I was going to miss it, so I asked them to remember our journey and the safe arrival of my mother from Beirut, Lebanon. I made sure that Paul, my son, joined me on this journey with his car tools, as he was capable of using them should we get into any problems!

We set off towards London Heathrow Airport to meet my mother off the aeroplane. This was my second journey to Heathrow Airport in my car, relying on Paul's sense of direction and following the map. While we were travelling on the M1, a major road to London, we met two young students, hitching a lift to London. We picked them up and a little later another African student also hitched a lift to London. We told them we were going to meet Mother at the airport and that she was coming from Beirut, Lebanon. This news caused them to ask me many questions.

They were asking me questions regarding Lebanon's political situation and I was only too glad to tell them how I was seeing the present situation from the biblical point of view. I believe Satan overheard the conversation and tried to interrupt. The steering wheel began to shake and judder and Paul suggested that we should stop and check the wheels. Paul had a good look at the four car wheels but could not detect anything wrong, so we all got back in and I drove another 12 to 13 metres. The shaking and juddering became much worse. We got out and had a closer look at the wheels.

This time, Paul noticed a large balloon-like bulging tyre on the back wheel and suggested changing the wheel. What a good thing that I had Paul and the students. They all joined in to help Paul change the wheel; they took off the faulty wheel and replaced it with a new one. What a relief, but as soon as we got in and started driving, minutes later, there was such an explosion! The car shook. I wondered what had happened. We thought someone had thrown something at our car as it was moving. In fact it was the faulty tyre exploding in the car boot.

What a mercy! It could have exploded in the face of the young men who were changing the wheel, or it could have exploded while we were in the car driving on the highway; this would have caused us to swerve into the ditch. I began counting our blessings. I was thankful it had happened during our outward journey and that Mother knew nothing about it. Had it happened after Mother got into the car, it could have caused my mother to fear cars even more.

When we got home, I thanked the church for their prayers. God had saved us from great danger that day. Praise His Name.

A rock stood as the hand of an angel

This incident reminds me of another narrow escape. John and I were going to visit elderly friends in North Wales. We had lost our way high up on the mountain and it had just started raining. We were trying to find our main road back and were coming down a steep hill. The car skidded down the steep road. I had no control over the car wheels or the brakes. The car left the road gliding onto the green meadow. I could hear and sense the bottom of the car scraping on stones. Eventually it stopped with a bit of help from the brake lever. I took a deep breath and prayed, while John began to blame me for not being able to stop the car. I put it into reverse gear and gently pressed on the accelerator. I was glad it moved backwards.

We both got out and examined the area. I found a stone, the size of a foot, concealed in the grass; it had stopped the car entering into the ditch below, where lambs were grazing.

To me that rock was like an angel's hand, put there by

God over the centuries to stop us falling into that ditch on that remote lonely country village road.

I was glad to close this episode by pulling the car onto the road and driving all the way to visit our friends, the Heards, in North Wales. It was lovely to see them, and have fellowship. After a prayer we left them and arrived home without any problem.

The arrival of my mother cheered me up. I had been anticipating this time with her for ages. The timing was just right – I had ample opportunity to care for her as I was not working any more and the family had gone to their respective studies.

Mother's wish was to see us but not to stay with us any longer than two weeks. She was hoping to go and stay with my sister in Canada, simply because they eat Armenian food and speak in Armenian. She had been to us years ago, when Timothy was about one year old, and she had tried then to get used to the English way of life, but she was unable to settle any longer than three months, even though I extended her stay.

However, because she was sent to England without a visa, the police were breathing down my neck, threatening to deport her back to Beirut, where she had no one left to care for her. The very fact of the police at my doorstep every now and again was causing a great deal of anxiety and fear for me. On top of this she used to say that she wished to die in Canada amongst her larger family.

We tried every possible means to get the British government to grant a visa or at least to allow this ailing elderly grand-mother to go to her other daughter in Canada, where she would be able to spend her twilight years in peace and dignity.

The British Consulate asked us for various documents, asked questions about her past and present life, her health and financial matters. There was endless red tape, that is to say she had to provide a clean bill of health certificate, X-ray of lungs and chest, a blood test and so on. All these had to be provided by the personnel who were employed by the Consulate; only their signature and examinations would be valid.

It was a full-time occupation for me to find all the addresses of the medical officer's clinics in Birmingham. We did our utmost to find them and make appointments. I would not have been able to find these places had I not had one of my sons, Samuel, to help drive us. Our GP also had to supply reports, which were sent together with the others to the British Consulate.

Twice my sister and her son Samuel came from Montreal to meet the British Consulate representative in an attempt to hasten the emigration procedures, but they were told it would take 48 months before anything could be done. We were devastated. In the end the Albarian family had to employ another solicitor to fight Mother's case for a visa to move to Canada to live with the Albarian family, her sons and 14 grandchildren.

Mother's desire was met 20 months later. My husband John and Daniel, our son, took Mother to her beloved daughter's home in Montreal.

She soon flourished. She always kept sweets in her possession to give to her grandchildren. Before long, she became the grandmother of all the members of the Armenian church in Montreal.

I was informed about my mother having a stroke in 1993. When I went to see her in hospital she saw me and gave me a wonderful smile, which I shall not forget. She was sadly missed by us and was known to everyone by her only English words, from the Gospel of John 3:16: "For God so loved the world that He gave His one and only Son, that whoever believes in Him shall not perish but have eternal life." She died on 10th February 1993. All her children and grandchildren were with her.

10

Visit to California in February, 1995

What I am about to share with you is about God's faithfulness to His Word.

> *"Delight yourself in the LORD and He will give you the desires of your heart."*
>
> Psalm 37:4

I have had many ambitions, most of them have been fulfilled by God's grace, apart from two, which have always been at the back of my mind. One desire was to see friends and relatives who have influenced my life and shaped my walk with the Lord, to thank them and to encourage them before it is too late, to tell them that their lives have brought good fruit into God's field. The second desire was to see my homeland, Armenia. I had heard so much about the country, the resilience of the people in keeping their faith in the risen Lord for over 1,700 years and their recent independence from the USSR after 70 years in exile.

One day I unexpectedly received a phone call from my eldest son, Daniel, who worked at Manchester Airport. He asked, "Mother, where would you like to go, Canada or California?"

I spontaneously said, "To California," because I have four cousins living in California and I had already been to Montreal in Canada two years earlier. Daniel added that Paul (his youngest brother) was already in California. Paul and Sam Albarian (two cousins) had crossed the land from Montreal to California, from east to west, by car. It had taken them eleven days travelling by land. Sam now lived in Montreal and was to start Bible college in California, where his brother, Rev Daniel Albarian, was already established as pastor in the Downey Buena Park area.

Arrangements were made, and Daniel, my son, took me to my nephew's house in Buena Park in California.

We had ten days of visiting several states. Paul drove us to Las Vegas. I call it sin city, Fresno. We met and fellowshipped with friends and relatives, drove to Sequoia and King Canyon National Park, then to Yosemite National Park and Los Angeles, to see the house where my husband's uncle used to live. He was a carpet merchant. Most of all we went to meet with Auntie Vergine Badeer in Ararat Home in Los Angeles. It was the Mission Hill residential home for retired Armenian citizens. The Ararat Home had been built by her husband Augustine Badeer's donation of their entire estate to the AMAA association in the form of a trust fund, and the income from it will support many worthy mission and service programmes for years to come.

Auntie Vergine was the person who had inspired me with her life and example. When she saw me with my sons, she reminded me of all those years ago. She called me her daughter and her memory was not diminished as some thought. However, I thanked her and we took her into the gardens of the Ararat Home, where we took a few pictures of us together.

My deepest desire was met in February, 1995.

Visit to Armenia in July, 1995

As I mentioned earlier, another of my desires was to see my motherland, Armenia, where Noah's Ark had rested on Mount Ararat.

Early in May 1995 I received another unexpected telephone call from my niece, Liza Albarian, in Canada. "Auntie, you have had a heart for mission work since your early teenage years, so I thought you would be interested in joining our youth group from Montreal. We will be going to Armenia for a month of mission work among needy Armenian children aged between seven and twelve. You could either come to Montreal or join us at Paris Charles De Gaulle Airport. I will send you all the details and plans."

It was a great surprise to know that my niece Liza had been interested in my desire and had thought of doing something about it! I told her that I would love to join them: "Let's pray about it. If it is the Lord's timing, all things will fall into place and the door will open for me to go to Armenia."

I telephoned my son, Samuel, in London, telling him what Liza had said on the phone about going to Armenia for a month of mission work. I asked him if he would be interested in joining me. Yes, Samuel did wish to join me and was prepared to take one month of annual leave. I also got in touch with my cousin, Hagop, who had lived in Armenia since the end of the Second World War. I remember waving goodbye to them at Beirut harbour. We had had practically no contact with Cousin Hagop for 50 years. We both had a double reason to go on this mission.

My son and I began preparing for this journey. Meanwhile I had been praying for God's guidance about what He wanted me to do once I got to Armenia.

By this time I had been living in Matlock since 1965, away from all Armenian communities. I had heard and read about Armenian people living in hardship through the representative of Christian Solidarity International, Baroness Cox, who "was well loved by the Armenians". She had highlighted the suffering of the innocent people of Nagorno Karabakh and people in Matlock had helped me to send gifts to the people in Nagorno Karabakh for Christmas 1994. Since then I had felt attached to the people in Hiyasdan.

Meanwhile my friend and I spent a day at a seminar in a Church of England church in the Clay Cross area. There I picked up a prayer book in which all the countries of the world were listed to be prayed for in churches. However, to my surprise, Armenia was not mentioned. This concerned me a lot and I lost sleep over it. How was it that Armenians had been forgotten? They needed all the more prayers! I thought that as there was a war between Azeries and Karabakh I would pray about this.

About two weeks later I heard of a Christian women's conference held in Hayes Conference Centre, Swanwick. It was 'The Lydia Fellowship International' conference and I was able to attend. There I found a large number of women from all over the world gathered to pray. Towards the end of this conference 160 national flags were held up, one flag between two or three ladies praying for that country specifically. I was anxious to trace if they had an Armenian flag. Yes, they had! Naturally, I was overwhelmed to find such a fellowship of ladies who were fasting and praying 'intercessory prayers'. It was at this meeting that I believe the Lord spoke to my heart. "I want you to take this 'Lydia Fellowship' into Armenia for the good of my people there." The title or motto of that day was: "Do whatever He tells you" (John 2:5).

By this time, I had already prepared to take a journey to Armenia, arranged by the First Armenian Evangelical Church in Montreal. My son and I enrolled with the group of volunteers who would be helping in the children's summer camp 1995, run by AMAA.

We departed from Manchester Airport on 29th June at 1.30pm. We flew on a British aeroplane to Paris Charles De Gaulle Airport. The journey to Paris was uneventful and when we arrived we met my niece Liza from Canada, together with Mrs Santourian and three Brazilian ladies who joined our team. In the luggage hall my niece was asked to pay $100 for excess luggage in spite of documents shown from recognised authorities. Mrs Santourian and I decided to pray and sent our 'SOS' to God. A few minutes later, I met the airport official with whom I had had a brief talk earlier. He said, "Just take the excess luggage up into the aeroplane with you." The first hurdle was over.

On the Armenian airline there were safety measures, but they were somewhat different from those we had encountered on the flight to Paris. Smoking was permitted in all areas and we were allowed to choose our seats. Meals were good and hygiene was observed.

After a five-hour flight from Paris we arrived at Armenia's capital Erevan (or Yerevan) airport at 1.30am. As our aeroplane touched down there was spontaneous hand clapping by all the travellers to show appreciation and thanks for our safe arrival. The airport was not as elegant as Charles De Gaulle. Everyone came off the plane onto the runway in total darkness and walked to the luggage hall. There we spent four stressful hours, anxiously looking to see if our belongings would appear on the turntable. There were no trolleys to put luggage on. Two men were standing clutching a trolley each – they were self-appointed porters. They loaded the trolleys so high that the luggage was almost touching the roof! Two metres away from the main exit there stood a petite lady highly made up, asking for between $20 and $30. We wondered if it was for airport tax! She then reduced her demand to half what she had asked for in the first place. When we asked her why she wanted so much money, she replied, "Armenia needs that money." I could not argue with that. In this place the lights would go off for several minutes, then on, then off. When we asked the reason why, they said, "To save electricity." In the twilight we all had to fill in a poorly printed form, hard to read and harder to understand. This was supposed to be the only formality.

There were no seats, no washrooms, and no drink dispensers. It was hot, so if you did not already know how to be patient, it was a good place to learn. It was so uncomfortable that people gave the fees they were asked for in order to escape through the large iron gates. At the end of four hours' waiting the luggage belonging to the Brazilian ladies in our team had still not appeared. Their luggage did not arrive until one week later, on the next flight from Paris. At about 6am, we were out of the airport compound.

Members of AMAA were waiting to take us to the centre, but my cousin, whom I had not seen for 50 years, had also been waiting all these long hours. He escorted us in his car, offering the most delicious refreshing apricots I have ever tasted. They are one of Armenia's most famous fruits.

As we entered the capital, Erevan, we saw here and there elderly ladies sweeping the streets. The town was still asleep and we felt as though we had been transported 100 years back in history. There were no colours, and the makeshift dwellings were dusty and rusty. However, we were all completely overwhelmed in wonder at seeing Mount Ararat some 60 miles away. It was rising as if it had been cut out of the sky, which was pink in the morning sunlight. It was an awesome sight. Although the temperature was getting on for 30 degrees centigrade in Erevan, the summit of Mount Ararat would remain snow-capped. This was where Noah's Ark was supposed to have rested (Genesis 8:4; 2 Kings 19:37; Isaiah 37:38; Jeremiah 51:27). Later, we saw in the city centre of Erevan surprisingly handsome buildings set among hills and green valleys.

The buildings were mostly of stone, and the architecture was of a solid, elegant, gothic style. The roads were pitted with potholes and there were overhead cables hanging everywhere. Some of them were for the city trams. We drove past a magnificent amphitheatre stadium set in the hillside (it was not in use), the Cognac distillery and the Sydney Opera House-style concert hall before arriving at the AMAA headquarters in Erevan. In the grounds was the mobile medical centre, a 40-foot trailer complete with all basic facilities. It even had a portable X-ray machine, but there was no electricity (it worked only with a generator). It had been donated following the 1988 earthquake. Doctor Samuel managed to take in the medicines brought from ECHO, including 10,000 multivitamins, water purification tablets, antibiotics and 300 tooth brushes for the children – a donation from a Matlock chemist.

There were burst water pipes in the streets. Repairs had long been neglected due to shortage of cash for public works. Unemployment, the four-year war and the Turkish and Azary blockade had all contributed to complete economic collapse, bringing 3.5 million Armenians to the brink of national disaster and threatening to kill thousands through the cold. As a result, trees had been cut down to keep families warm through the bitter winters. Now the war had stopped, yet there was still no proper electricity supply, only for a few hours a day. The post office was unreliable; television, radio and telephone communications were still interrupted and there was no fuel for heating water, because the water supply pumps lacked force. Some refugees were still living in metal tanks, which had previously been used for the transport of petrol.

Once I was in the office of the AMAA headquarters I plucked up courage to share what the Lord had put in my heart. The Lord had said to me before leaving England for Armenia, "I want you to take Lydia Fellowship into Armenia for the good of my people there." I shared this thought with the leaders of AMAA (Evangelical pastors). The Lydia Fellowship intercessors believe in fasting and praying. When believing women pray and fast for people in authority, God will help and change situations. "If my people, who are called by my name, will humble themselves and pray and seek my face and turn from their wicked ways, then will I hear from heaven and will forgive their sin and will heal their land" (2 Chronicles 7:14). I believed this was God's strategy. His Word holds. Praise Him.

On Saturday 1st July we were in a van, on our way through a mountain pass to the summer camp which was somewhere high up in the mountains. It was supposed to be an idyllic place for camping on the outskirts of Vanatzor, formerly known as Girovagan. (Since Armenian independence in 1991, some towns had changed their names.) It was a beautiful city in the mountains, the people were kind and hospitable and the summer campsite was two hours away by car from the capital, Erevan. The campers were housed in two large buildings. The first camp included 325 children and 40 leaders, most of them Sunday school teachers from several towns, plus kitchen staff and visiting helpers from Canada, California, Brazil, France, Lebanon and England.

The year 1995 was no exception. During the months of July and August more than 1,500 children experienced ten days of camp activities at Vanatzor, where the AMAA, through the local Armenian Evangelical Church, rented a campsite for two months. The children were grouped by age and participated in camp programmes appropriate for their age group. These included sports, outdoor recreation, cultural activities, handicrafts and Christian education.

They were mostly well behaved. There was a spirit of love,

harmony and friendship, which prevailed throughout, especially among those of us coming from different lands. One Brazilian lady said, "God has chosen us and brought us all together to minister to the spiritual needs of the children." We felt the Spirit of the Lord at work in their tender lives and they were very attentive to the Bible teaching. They could recite, sing and play. It was a sheer joy to see them put all their heart and soul into their activities. They were hungry for food, not only physical but also spiritual food. At the end of the first ten days of summer camp, 50 children stood on the platform declaring Christ Jesus as their Lord and Saviour. I rushed to give them Luke's gospel and congratulated them with a hug and a kiss. As they were singing, my heart was bouncing with joy, as I knew there was joy in heaven over one sinner who repented. I encouraged them with the fact that their names were now written in the Book of Life, and that they were children of God. God was their 'Abba' father, who would never leave nor forsake them. They had to trust God in all things, seek His will and be obedient to His Word, and all the rest would be added to them (Matthew 6:33).

A young Christian gentleman by the name of Mihran Shlougian, born in Armenia but living in New York for the past ten years, had come back to Armenia bringing with him Christian literature to distribute. I asked him to give me as many as he could spare because I had run out of my own literature, and I distributed them all to the boys and girls in the camp.

There was a lady doctor in the camp. Her name was Nazely and she was very kind and able, full of talent. Doctor Samuel was asked to check the heart and lungs of every child. He found a few abnormalities and notified the authorities. Quite a few children suffered from toothache and some of them had very bad teeth, needing extensive dental treatment. On the whole no serious illness was encountered.

At the end of each camp all the children were given gift parcels, containing practical items such as T-shirts, shoes, school materials, toothbrushes, pads and paper, copybooks and so on. Three large buses transported the children safely to their homes.

Churches were full to overflowing; people were hungry for more of God's Word. The Holy Spirit was active in changing people's lives. We in the West are concerned with empty pews but their pews are not empty, the problem was having enough seats and space. One Sunday I was at the AMAA headquarters church where 15 adults gave their lives anew to Jesus.

What about their hospitality? They were so glad to receive from other countries guests who identified with their suffering. They gave their best (like the widow's mite) and borrowed from neighbours if they didn't have enough, so it became a community feast. Our hearts melted to see and experience their love, unity and joy. After each meal they put a lively folk dance tape on and began to rejoice. Everyone took part in the dancing.

After returning home I was given permission by Mrs Shelagh McAlpine, the International Co-ordinator, to translate the Lydia Fellowship literature* into Armenian. (Sadly she died in 2005.)

It took two years to translate the Lydia Fellowship pamphlets. Shelagh's daughter helped to raise $400 for the printing and she herself brought it to England. I sent translated Lydia Fellowship introductory letters to 75 Armenian Evangelical churches round the world. The rest of the literature has been taken to Armenia by the Pambakian's Armenian Ministries for distribution amongst the churches in Armenia and to raise an army of intercessors for our nation. The only way of dismantling the bad is by prayers (1 Timothy 2:1-2).

I have had very little feedback since but I am trusting in His unfailing Word. It shall not return to Him void.

Surprise visit back to my birth place

Recently, in 2002, I had the opportunity to visit my birthplace, to see my niece and her family.

I had an unexpected call from my son, Daniel, urging me to get ready to fly to Beirut. When I asked how this idea had come about, he said, "You always said you wished to visit Beirut, your birthplace again, before it was too late. So when I

---

*Lydia Fellowship International, PO Box 566, 40 Pembroke Street, Oxford OX1 1WU, UK

had a few days free, I got air tickets for both of us. We are to fly this weekend, 10am from Heathrow Airport."

"It's very short notice, I have other plans." I was nervous to commit myself at first, because that night I had had a very bad dream and my mind was full of fears. I tried to find an excuse not to accept the offer.

Daniel got cross and put the phone down on me. I thought, "Now I have upset him by rejecting his kind offer of accompanying me on this flight to Beirut."

I got down on my knees and prayed, "Lord, what's going on? I have upset my son." The bad dream was dominating my thoughts and there was a special Lay Weekend at the church, which I was looking forward to attending. As I was praying my thoughts got clearer – I had to put aside my own agenda and put my son's first. As I thought this, peace of mind came to me. I went back immediately, picked up the phone and rang Daniel. When he answered, I apologised and thanked him for being so kind. He had remembered what I had said in the past, and he had put it in his heart to please me. I thanked God for him.

At Heathrow Airport we sat in the aeroplane waiting over an hour for the airspace communications engineer to arrive, who was late. When eventually he arrived he had to check the radar system before we could fly. When we asked the hostess why we were waiting she explained the reason. Daniel knew exactly what to do because he was trained in this line of engineering, but because he was a passenger he could not help. The flight took off.

After five-and-a-half hours of flying we touched down at 10pm at Beirut Airport where my niece, Arousiag, her husband and their two sons welcomed us. We were whisked off to the mountainous area where they had their house. We were told the car was a new one – their old car had been stolen a few days before.

We thanked God for our safe arrival. After the preliminary exchange of news we were shown to our beds and had a good night's sleep. The following day they took us to see most of the tourist sights that are worth seeing, including some of the world's seven wonders – the Jeita Grotto Upper

Gallery and Lower Gallery of stalactites and stalagmites, the Cedars of Lebanon, 4,000-year-old Byblos, Sidon and Baalbac.

On the Sunday we went to my school church. The only few seats available were next to my school class teacher. She turned and looked to see who was sitting down beside her. She spontaneously said, "Where did you spring from? You are Ovsanna Bedrossian." I blinked at her. After the service we had Turkish coffee in disposable cups. My ex-pastor Hagop's widow, Mrs Ellen Sagherian, introduced me to some of the folk. So many new faces – so much had changed. (Ellen's husband, Rev Hagop, had been instrumental in my coming to England). They had gone through 17 years of civil war, yet had also been building and extending both the church and the school.

Mrs Ellen and my niece, Arousiag, had arranged together to give me a surprise invitation to a banquet (dinner party) in a hotel, which was being held to celebrate the 80th anniversary of the Central High School. Each ticket was £20. Mrs Ellen had paid for me. This was organised by the Parent Teacher Association, to raise money for the students whose parents are unable to pay for their child's school fees.

They had a clever way of raising sums of money for the CHS. Each parent had to donate some things that could be resold by auction. There was also 'bring and buy', works of art that could be sold, cakes and so on. It was done in a big way. They had invited musicians from Armenia – a violinist and vocalist. Games and quizzes also took place.

The platform was decorated with flowers, and appetising Armenian dinners were served. Then there was a presentation, and the school anthem was sung. There was a large birthday cake with 80 candles and sparklers that were lit, followed by thanks and rewards given to those teachers who had served in the school for 25 to 30 years.

In the middle of all this, the principal announced my name as a distinguished guest from England, an ex-pupil, representing Miss Alice Albarian who had served as deputy principal and Sunday school teacher, for over 30 years. Because Alice was in Montreal at the time and I happened to be there, they called me onto the platform, presented me with a large bouquet of flowers and kissed my cheeks three times (a local custom). Miss Alice Albarian is my sister's sister-in-law, so I was closely related to her. I was so overwhelmed – who was I to receive all this fuss?

They took pictures, which will be in the school history (metaphorically speaking). I felt like Mephibosheth (2 Samuel 9:6-13). I am grateful for all the love and hospitality I received during my visit to the Armenian Evangelical Central High School. It was good to see them and renew nostalgic memories of years gone by.

When I stopped and considered all that the Lord had done, when I was feeling downcast, lonely, isolated from all my friends and family, God knew how to bring smiles back to me, that is why I called it God's favour.

Looking back to the start of this visit, when I was so reluctant to commit myself to Daniel's offer of an air flight to Beirut with him, I realised that this was God's doing. I needed an emotional uplift at the time. This visit to Beirut was so timely, not only for myself but also for my niece and her two young sons. I was able to share with them how the Lord of my life had guided, protected and provided. All praise to Jesus.

Parental duty calls to Rhode Island twice and to Massachusetts

The Allen family was blessed by the birth of our first grandson, Joshua Nathan, on 3rd November 2000, to Yvonne and Paul. Beautiful baby Rebecca Joy, born 21st February 2003, two years later, was sister to Joshua and our first granddaughter.

Grandma could not wait to see the precious gifts of life from the Lord. I endeavoured to give a helping hand to Yvonne and Paul as they were busy with their respective work and study. Since Paul's graduation it was paramount that they should find a place to call their own home. They saw potential in an old house and put in an offer to purchase it. The renovation work was horrendous, therefore it was essential for me to go and help look after the children some of the time, after their return from nursery. Whilst I was there, Paul was selected as pastor of a Full Gospel Church in Boston Massachusetts. I had the pleasure of being present at his induction.

Retirement – or rather the start of new service

Now I am on a journey to discover God's greater plans for my life. In the past couple of years, I got involved in computer lessons to satisfy my curiosity to discover how computers work. At the same time I endeavoured to improve my English language, reading and writing skills. When we met at the Ritz Centre, the teacher suggested that we should have 'Matlock town' as our project. This reminded me of my early teenage years, when I was living in Beirut, Lebanon. As a young child I was making castles in the air, as it were, when two significant occurrences happened, which I believe were the preludes for my living in Matlock.

Here are the accounts of these occurrences:

My brother Jacob purchased a second-hand gramophone, which also included two long-playing gramophone records. One side of this record had the popular song called 'Johnny is the Boy For Me'. I am sure some of you may remember this song, which went like this: 'Johnny is the boy for me, I knew that it would be. Yes, my darling, I replied, Johnny is the boy for me, I knew that it would be!'

The second side of the record was the British National Anthem, 'God Save the Queen'. Each day on my return home from school, I would play the record on the old gramophone and sing at the top of my voice, with the windows wide open, amusing myself with ambitious dreams...

Another incident I remembered took place at school in a geography lesson. We were learning about England; the teacher hung up a large map of England and pointed out the area of Derbyshire on the map and said, "This area is away from surrounding sea coasts, being in the centre of England. Due to it's position the people suffer with a condition called 'Goitre', also known as 'Derbyshire neck'. This is due to lack of or excess of thyroid hormone. In addition, rickets were common amongst the children. A disorder of calcium and phosphorus metabolism associated with a deficiency of vitamin D.

Meanwhile I was daydreaming, thinking that it would be great if I had a boyfriend called Johnny in Derbyshire! Was I prophesying? I do not know, but God knows.

My geography teacher also asked us to look around and find some things within our houses that were imported goods from England, or made in England. I remember finding a few cotton bobbins, made in Cromford near Matlock and exported as far as Beirut, Lebanon. In fact, those manufactured cotton reels have gone to all four corners of the world. The factory in Cromford Mill was the world's first successful water-powered cotton spinning mill. In was in the 18th century that Richard Arkwright devised modern factory production techniques. The site has been going through extensive restoration in recent years. My neighbour, Mr Charlton, is a historian and, together with others, has succeeded in naming the Derwent Valley mill in Derbyshire as a world heritage site. In December 2001 the mill was added to the UNESCO (United Nations Educational, Scientific and Cultural Organisation) world heritage centres.

I arrived in England to study nursing and then midwifery. In my first week at the King Edward Memorial Hospital, I was introduced to another Armenian lady called Verkiné from Damascus, Syria. She had graduated from the same hospital as I had in Ealing, London. We soon became good friends and, six months later, we decided to have a week of holiday at the Keswick Convention at Westmoreland Lake District. We were travelling by train. (The trains used to run past Matlock up to Manchester and beyond in those days.) As we were approaching Matlock, people in the train were so excited with the beauty of the surrounding countryside. They all got off their seats to gaze out of the windows; we, too, joined the excitement and looked out of the window. It never occurred to me that one day I would settle and make my home in this beautiful area of Matlock. These were God's pointers; the start of things to come. The memories, which had escaped my mind, were revived when the teacher suggested writing a project about Matlock.

Is there trouble anywhere?

What a Friend I have in Jesus,
All my sins and griefs to bear!
What a privilege to carry
Everything to God in prayer!
O what peace I often forfeit,
O what needless pain I bear,
All because I do not carry
Everything to God in prayer!

Have I had trials and temptations?
Is there trouble anywhere?
I should never be discouraged:
Take it to the Lord in prayer.
Can I find a friend so faithful,
Who will all my sorrows share?
Jesus knows my every weakness:
Take it to the Lord in prayer.

I am weak and heavy-laden,
'Cumbered with a load of care.
Precious Saviour, still my refuge:
I will take it to the Lord in prayer.
Do my friends despise, forsake me?
I will take it to the Lord in prayer;
In His arms He'll take and shield me,
I will find a solace there.

Joseph Scriven (adapted)

Trust and Obey

When we walk with the Lord in the light of His Word,
What a glory He sheds on our way!
While we do His good will, He abides with us still,
And with all who will trust and obey.

Chorus:
Trust and obey, for there's no other way
To be happy in Jesus, but to trust and obey.

Not a shadow can rise, not a cloud in the skies,
But His smile quickly drives it away;
Not a doubt or a fear, not a sigh or a tear,
Can abide while we trust and obey.

Not a burden we bear, not a sorrow we share,
But our toil He doth richly repay;
Not a grief or a loss, not a frown or a cross,
But is blessed if we trust and obey.

But we never can prove the delights of His love
Until all on the altar we lay;
For the favour He shows, for the joy He bestows,
Are for them who will trust and obey.

Then in fellowship sweet we will sit at His feet,
Or we'll walk by His side in the way;
What He says we will do, where He sends we will go;
Never fear, only trust and obey.

John H Sammis and Daniel B Towner, 1887
(from the Nazarene Hymnal)

11

History of Armenia in a nutshell

Armenia (Hayastan) has always centred around the biblical Mount Ararat, Southern Caucasus. Haik, the legendary father of the Armenians, challenged the authority of Belus, the tyrant despot of Babylon, slew him in combat, gathered his family and settled on what was later known as the home of the Armenians. This was the beginning of the Armenian state, 1200 BC.

The Armenian tradition maintains that they are direct descendants of Armais or Aramais, the grandson of the Armenian hero and patriach Haik 2350 BC, who descended from Noah's son, Japheth.

Since the beginning of Armenia's history, from 2350 BC, and her documented statehood, beginning in the 9th century BC, Armenia has been overrun by invaders and looted and ravaged many times. Yet after each subjugation Armenia has rebuilt her devastated country and regained her independence or autonomy. Assyria, Babylonia, the Medes, Achaemenid Persia, Alexander the Great, the Romans, the Byzantines, Arabs, Seljuke and Turks have invaded Armenia, but none has been able to crush the independent spirit of her people.

When the Persian King 'Hazgerd' ordered the Armenians to become fire-worshippers, they replied, "No one can dislodge us from this faith, neither angels nor men, not even the fire or the sword or any horrible torture... your sword and our necks."

Vartan Mamigonian, the commander-in-chief of the Armenian army, led his men to the battlefield of Avarair – "in the name of our fatherland and our faith in Christ Jesus, forward". At his side was Ghevont Yeretz, cross in hand, the representative of the Armenian Church. This was the first war in history to be waged in defence of the Christian faith and it was fought in 451 AD. The Vartanantz War has been commemorated annually for over 1,554 years in Armenian churches worldwide.

(Pre-Christian belief followed the Iranian Zoroastrian pattern.)

The story of the young Saint Gregory the Illuminator

It was 287 AD. This young man, Gregory, had fallen out of favour with the king, Dertad (or Trdat) III, and had been exiled from the country; but in exile he had heard the Christian message. At last, in spite of the risk, he decided to come back to share the Gospel with his countrymen.

The king soon learned of his return and had him seized and thrown into the deepest 40-foot dungeon of the castle to die of starvation, but not before the king's sister had listened to Gregory's preaching and become a believer. The young woman strode down the dark stone stairs to the black, foul-smelling dungeon, hiding a loaf of bread and a gourd of goat's milk beneath her cloak. For 14 years she managed to keep the saint alive.

At that point a dreadful malady seized the king, a strange insanity that hurled him to the floor grunting like an animal. During his lucid moments he asked his physicians to heal him, but no one could.

"The man Gregory could help you," his sister suggested.

"Gregory died many years ago," the king retorted. "His bones are rotting beneath this very castle."

"He is alive," she said and described her 14-year vigil. So Gregory was brought from the dungeon, his hair as white as the snow on Mount Ararat, but sound in mind and spirit.

"In the name of Jesus Christ," he rebuked the demon tormenting the king, and in that instant the king was healed.

In the year 301 AD, King Dertad (or Trdat) III and Saint Gregory set out to achieve the conversion of all Armenians, making it the first ever Christian nation state.

St Gregory the Illuminator had been locked away for 14 years, but had never lost faith, never lost hope, waited only for God's perfect time...

According to legend, Armenia is supposed to have been visited by the apostles Bartholomew and Thaddeus about 20 years after Christ's crucifixion.

The Encyclopaedia Britannica throws more light by saying that in the Bible it is said that certain Greeks, who came to enquire, "'Sir... we would like to see Jesus,'" (John 12:21) prior to Jesus' suffering, were Armenian delegates.

The golden age of the Armenian alphabet was in 405-6 AD when two outstanding clergymen, Sahak and Mesrop (Mashdos), started the task of translating the Bible into Armenian. The first Armenian Bible was printed in Amsterdam in 1666 AD.

The land of Armenia

Armenia is a high mountainous country about the size of Belgium; it covers an area of 11,490 square miles and is an average of 5,900 feet above sea level.

Although the Tigris, Euphrates and Araxes rivers originate in Armenia, none is navigable. Farmers call their land, "land of stones". There are 900 alpine peaks and 20 mountain ranges and the central plateau is windswept and arid. Temperatures can go up to 42°C in summer. Winter temperatures go down to -12°C.

Mount Ararat is 13,419 feet high. Armenians have great pride and sense of identity in this powerful symbol they call 'Masis' at the heart of the ancient kingdom of greater Armenia. Yet the Turkish border now separates the Armenian people from their mountain. Now only one tenth of the land is theirs. It used to stretch to southwest Cilicia in Turkey, where the Apostle Paul was born. Until 1991 it was one of the smallest of the 15 USSR republics.

Prayer

If you would like to begin a personal relationship with Jesus today, please pray this:

> *"Lord Jesus, I invite you into my life. I believe you died for me and that your blood pays for my sins and provides me with the gift of eternal life. By faith I receive that gift and I acknowledge you as my Lord and Saviour. Amen."*

If you have prayed this prayer and really mean it, here are the next steps to take:

- Find a church where the Bible is preached and start to attend regularly. Tell the minister what you have prayed.

- Talk to God in prayer every day, just as you would to a loving earthly father.

- Start to read the Bible for yourself. It is a good idea to start at the New Testament. A version in modern day language, like the New International Version, may be helpful at first.

Remember you will be like a little toddler starting the Christian walk in life. If you 'fall', get up and keep going. God will help you if you ask Him.

> *"Now to Him who is able to do immeasurably more than all we ask or imagine, according to His power that is at work within us, to Him be glory in the church and in Christ Jesus throughout all generations, for ever and ever! Amen."*
> Ephesians 3:20-21

His appearance is like Lebanon, choice as its cedars.
(Song of Solomon 5:15b)

His mouth is sweetness itself; he is altogether lovely.
This is my lover, this my friend, O daughters of Jerusalem.
(Song of Solomon 5:16)

Again I ask: Did they stumble so as to fall beyond recovery? Not at all! Rather, because of their transgression, salvation has come to the Gentiles to make Israel envious. But if their transgression means riches for the world, and their loss means riches for the Gentiles, how much greater riches will their fullness bring!

I am talking to you Gentiles. Inasmuch as I am the apostle to the Gentiles, I make much of my ministry in the hope that I may somehow arouse my own people to envy and save some of them. For if their rejection is the reconciliation of the world, what will their acceptance be but life from the dead? If the part of the dough offered as firstfruits is holy, then the whole batch is holy; if the root is holy, so are the branches.

If some of the branches have been broken off, and you, though a wild olive shoot, have been grafted in among the others and now share in the nourishing sap from the olive root, do not boast over those branches. If you do, consider this: You do not support the root, but the root supports you. You will say then, "Branches were broken off so that I could be grafted in." Granted. But they were broken off because of unbelief, and you stand by faith. Do not be arrogant, but be afraid. For if God did not spare the natural branches, he will not spare you either.

Consider therefore the kindness and sternness of God: sternness to those who fell, but kindness to you, provided that you continue in his kindness. Otherwise, you also will be cut off. And if they do not persist in unbelief, they will be grafted in, for God is able to graft them in again. After all, if you were cut out of an olive tree that is wild by nature, and contrary to nature were grafted into a cultivated olive tree, how much more readily will these, the natural branches, be grafted into their own olive tree!

(Romans 11:11-24)

Ovsanna Allen

Ovsanna Allen (known to her friends as 'Hosanna') is an Armenian. Like all other Armenian families, they were forced to leave their homes by the Turkish Gendarmes.

This is a story of what God can do with a life that is surrendered completely to Him.

In this book Ovsanna writes about the way in which God led her, the daughter of refugees who fled to Beirut, Lebanon, by picking her out of unforeseen protracted civil war situations in Beirut – as it were on the wings of an eagle – and set her on safer land. Protected, provided and promised.

> *"The God of all grace, who called you to His eternal glory in Christ, after you have suffered a little while, will Himself restore you and make you strong, firm and steadfast."*
> 1 Peter 5:10

Ovsanna wrote this book mainly to give thanks to the Lord, to call on His name, to make known among the nations what He has done, and to declare that His name is exalted (Isaiah 12:4).

God blessed Ovsanna and settled her as a mother and grandmother. She is now living in Matlock, Derbyshire.

All glory due to Him!